Jess Franco on filmmaking:

"I never made a film thinking that I'd win the Grand Prize in Cannes. Never. I always thought it would be so beautiful for my films to be shown in theaters in the suburbs and the theater is packed with people who are enjoying my films. There it is. That's more than enough. There's nothing else."

"I'm not a false intellectual like so many in the business. But I think that cinema is an art form in itself. It's an artistic expression that, let's say, makes the public happy."

"I feel that cinema should be like a box of surprises, like a magic box. And in that world, anything is allowed to enter, as long as it's always treated with a spirit of 'Pop!' Not in the spirit of 'Now you understand the problems of society in 1947.' No, I don't give a shit about that. I think cinema should be like magic, a surprise, that's all."

"I think a censor is a kind of dictator. The thing is so old-fashioned. They try to cut our wings. It's a pain in the ass. I hate that. I like freedom. I have always liked freedom. I left Spain because I liked freedom... What does it all mean? Who is the judge? Who decides? Who has the truth? Who holds the truth with a capital 'T'? No one! So there's nothing worse than bullshit that cuts people's wings."

BIBLIOGRAPHY

Horror is Art! (2015)
Film Phreak Speaks! (2015)
Film Phreak Speaks! Part Two: The Revenge (2015)
F*cked Up Fiction Vol. One (2015)
Notes from the Noir Journal Volume 1
(2015; co-authored with Ann Snuggs)

JESS FRANCO:
The World's Most Dangerous Filmmaker

Kristofer Todd Upjohn

Stark House Press • Eureka California

JESS FRANCO: THE WORLD'S MOST DANGEROUS FILMMAKER

Published by Stark House Press
1315 H Street
Eureka, CA 95501
griffinskye3@sbcglobal.net
www.starkhousepress.com

JESS FRANCO: THE WORLD'S MOST DANGEROUS FILMMAKER
Copyright © 2018 by Kristofer Todd Upjohn. All rights reserved, including the right of reproduction in whole or in part in any form. Published by Stark House Press by arrangement with the author.

ISBN-13: 978-1-944520-60-1

Layout by Mark Shepard, SHEPGRAPHICS.COM
Cover design from a poster for *La Malediction de Frankenstein*
from Fenix Film (Madrid)
Proofreading by Bill Kelly

PUBLISHER'S NOTE
This is a work of fiction. Names, characters, places and incidents are either the products of the author's imagination or used fictionally, and any resemblance to actual persons, living or dead, events or locales, is entirely coincidental.
Without limiting the rights under copyright reserved above, no part of this publication may be reproduced, stored, or introduced into a retrieval system or transmitted in any form or by any means (electronic, mechanical, photocopying, recording or otherwise) without the prior written permission of both the copyright owner and the above publisher of the book.

First Stark House Press Edition: April 2018

FIRST EDITION

TABLE OF CONTENTS

INTRODUCTION 9
CHRISTINA, PRINCESS OF EROTICISM 13
THE DIABOLICAL DR. Z (1966) 22
COUNT DRACULA (1970) 28
BLOODY MOON (1981) 35
EUGENIE (1969) 40
DRACULA, PRISONER OF FRANKENSTEIN (1972) 45
VAMPYROS LESBOS (1971) 50
99 WOMEN (1969) 56
LUST FOR FRANKENSTEIN (1998) 62
OASIS OF THE ZOMBIES (1983) 67
EXORCISM (1975) 71
DAUGHTER OF DRACULA (1972) 75
TENDER FLESH (1997) 80
FEMALE VAMPIRE (1973) 83
THE DEMONS (1973) 89
JACK THE RIPPER (1976) 95
THE BLOOD OF FU MANCHU (1968) 98
WOMEN BEHIND BARS (1975) 101
DEVIL HUNTER (1980) 104
THE AWFUL DR. ORLOFF (1962) 107
VENUS IN FURS (1969) 110
BLUE RITA (1977) 113
THE BLOODY JUDGE (1970) 115
MANSION OF THE LIVING DEAD (1982) 118
LOVE LETTERS OF A PORTUGUESE NUN (1977) 120
ATTACK OF THE ROBOTS (1966) .123
THE EROTIC RITES OF FRANKENSTEIN (1972) 125

THE SEX IS CRAZY (1981) 128
ILSA THE WICKED WARDEN (1977) 130
SHE KILLED IN ECSTASY (1970) 135
JUSTINE (1969) 139
WOMEN IN CELLBLOCK 9 (1976) .142
THE CASTLE OF FU MANCHU (1969) 144
NIGHT HAS A THOUSAND DESIRES (1984) 146
FACELESS (1987) 148
EUGÉNIE DE SADE (1973) 150
BARBED WIRE DOLLS (1976) 152
HOW TO SEDUCE A VIRGIN (1973) 154
THE SINISTER EYES OF DR. ORLOFF (1973) 157
LORNA THE EXORCIST (1974) 159
NIGHTMARES COME AT NIGHT (1972) 160
REVENGE IN THE HOUSE OF USHER (1983) 162
THE SADISTIC BARON VON KLAUS (1962) 164
THE HOT NIGHTS OF LINDA (1975) 169
COUNTESS PERVERSE (1974) 172
APPENDIX: ZOMBIE LAKE 176
FILMOGRAPHY 183

Dedicated to
Ann Snuggs, Karl Kaefer,
Steven Ronquillo, Tim Lucas and
Robert Stoll of Super Strange Video

INTRODUCTION

A story is told that the Roman Catholic Church declared Jess Franco to be the world's most dangerous filmmaker. If I was a director (and cinematographer, writer, actor, etc., as was Franco), I would take such an accusation as a tremendous compliment. Cesar Cruz said, "Art should comfort the disturbed and disturb the comfortable." Franco certainly did that.

Franco's frequently transgressive cinema certainly lives up to that of someone who is described as the world's most dangerous filmmaker. This director's films are wonderlands and dreamscapes for all us progressive weirdos. His movies are certainly boundary shattering. For many, Franco's films are certainly discomfiting. As does Cruz, I believe that a key function of art is to stretch the envelope. This stretching helps us grow as individuals and as a society.

Spaniard filmmaker Jesús Franco Manera was born on May 12, 1930 and died on April 2, 2013, as the result of a stroke. Between those dates he created a profusion of films, a few of which would not raise too many eyebrows, but many of which would go on to generate storms of controversy. At least for those who saw them. The director's work was the outside-of-Hollywood cinematic answer to "Off-Off-Broadway" plays. Not only did Franco work mostly in Europe, but he also made the type of movie that stood little chance of gaining mainstream acceptance.

Franco's films were shot on the cheap (though he knew how to pack in maximum production value per dollar spent) and they frequently involved graphic sexuality, sadism and edgy horror themes. In this book, I discuss a recurring theme in the director's work: the heady intersection of death (Thanatos) and eroticism (Eros). As this theme reoccurs consistently in Franco's catalogue, I will be revisiting it at some length in this book.

Sigmund Freud might have had some questionable ideas, at least in retrospect, but his assertion that Eros and Thanatos are two driving, primal forces in human psychology is indisputably true. As such, it should come as no shock to find these ideas explored profoundly in the work of Jess Franco. Of course, shock is abundant in his films, sometimes even for those of us who have already consumed some of the director's work. Newcomers are in for a hell of a surprise—and in for a treat if their soul is not governed by prudishness.

Prudery has no place in Franco's work.

This is a volume of film criticism, not a biography. Biographical information of course can be found elsewhere if the reader is curious. This book is instead a collection of essays analyzing many of the director's most important and significant films, as well as a few of his lesser known efforts. The exact number of movies in Franco's filmography cannot be readily determined. Estimates range from around 150 to more than 200! The reason for this uncertainty is partly attributable to the fact that multiple versions of several of his films are known to exist, although this creation of multiple versions was not always of Franco's doing. This multiple version phenomenon is a curiosity I will discuss further.

Each chapter of *The World's Most Dangerous Filmmaker* covers a film from Franco's oeuvre. I discuss not only the plots of each film, but I also explore the deeper metatextual layers lying within each of these works. Some movies receive a deeper, heavier discussion than others. Some chapters are rather long while some are on the short side. There is no pattern: the level of detail each film receives is simply a matter of the film in question and my reaction to it.

The order in which I cover the movies also follows no pattern. I didn't wish to cover them chronologically simply because some of his earlier movies are less interesting, frankly, than the more progressive cinema the director came to specialize in later. So I have mixed things up—just like Franco himself. You will find chapters on classic gothic films bumping up against some of the filmmaker's most notorious shockers.

That said, the reader should feel free to jump around. I do occasionally refer to something mentioned in a previous chapter, but hopefully no confusion should ensue. And if the reader chooses to read the chapters out of order (and chronologically speaking the chapters are "out-of-order", anyway!), and encounters a reference to a topic discussed in a previously unread chapter, then the reader, if so inclined, can refer to the chapter he or she has yet to read.

Although none of these movies are new, they will of course be new to those who have not yet seen Franco's films. So it behooves me to mention that there are spoilers, since in some of these chapters I will discuss the movie's plot in some detail. However, my job is not that of a film critic reviewing a movie, who will share his or her opinions, but will be obliged not to share plot outcomes.

Rather, I will be sharing analytical film criticism such as you might find in a college film class—hopefully, Jess Franco movies are being taught or will soon be taught in university classes. I'm interested in discussing his films as art. Of course, I also hope that my readers will include some newcomers to the world of Jess Franco and that my

INTRODUCTION

words will serve to encourage them to jump from my book to the movies themselves.

The films of Jess Franco are exceptionally challenging. The more constricted are one's personal boundaries, the more apt these boundaries are to fall like the walls of Jericho—assuming the viewer doesn't run away screaming. But as indicated by the quote from Cesar Cruz above, that is exactly the reaction his art should provoke. I hope this book challenges the reader to seek out the even greater challenges to be discovered in Franco's cinematic art.

CHRISTINA, PRINCESS OF EROTICISM (1973)

Spanish art house auteur Jess Franco spent much of his career using cinema to explore the intersection of death (Thanatos) and eroticism (Eros). His mastery of conceptual surrealism appears again and again in his work.

In Franco's oeuvre, sex and death nearly always intersect with each other in ways more subversive than just the basic transgression of crossing the two to begin with. And this counter-traditional dovetailing of Thanatos and Eros is usually, in Franco's canon, packaged in experiential films that will use a basic plot idea and expand it conceptually.

Jess Franco was, by and large, an artist more interested in ideas both big and intimate than in strict, conventional storytelling. His mystical approach to love, sex and death had more room to maneuver in the director's preferred style of elliptical cinema.

Christina, Princess of Eroticism (aka *A Virgin Among the Living Dead*) is, in every way, one of the finest expressions of Franco's style and ideas. His distinctive surrealism and his unique focus on the shadowy ways in which sex and death interact with each other are both in peak form in this film.

This film is a fan favorite and one of my own beloved Franco films. The director himself ranked this film among his most cherished works.

Sometimes opening credits can be intriguing. Such is particularly the case with the opening section of *Christina, Princess of Eroticism*. Jess Franco's movies are nearly always accompanied by curious scores that help set the strange moods permeating his films. The noteworthy Bruno Nicolai, who scored many European genre films, puts us on edge as he hypnotizes us with the tense music that plays over the credits. Our perspective is from a moving car. The footage it graces immerses us in the film. *Christina* possesses of one of the finest scores to grace a Franco film. This is immediately apparent with the avant-garde jazz music that accompanies us into the tenebrous erotic world the film inhabits.

In story terms, we witness the lead character Christina's trip to Montserrate, the family estate to which she has been summoned due to a relative's illness and impending death. On a deeper level, this camera perspective includes us in the journey, making the viewer a participant, not a mere spectator. Combined with Nicolai's music, this "cinematic movement" is an eerie transition into an otherworldly place.

If your goal is the old family estate, don't let anybody stop you. Go there!

That is the message delivered from a wise woman to the film's female lead, the mondo-sexy Christina Benton, played by Christina von Blanc (here credited as Cristine von Blanc). The film's luscious protagonist is on her way back to the familial homestead to visit her dying Aunt Abigail (Rosa Palomar).

The dialogue begins after Christina's arrival at a small-town inn where she is to meet her ride out to the big house in the country.

The reassurance provided by the wise woman is welcome, because when Christina first tells the innkeeper that she is visiting family—and the house where her family calls home—he fires off a superstition-laden response, warning the young woman that nobody ever goes there: Christina is bound for her doom.

In Christina's mind, however, she's simply going home.

(The editor of *Video Watchdog*, Tim Lucas, views the film as a study in depression, as he states in his commentary for the Redemption Films release of the movie. He makes a number of excellent arguments for this interpretation, one of them being that this innkeeper with questions is actually wearing the outfit of a doctor and is busy taking notes on what Christina says. (The reader is strongly encouraged to view the movie with Lucas' commentary.)

At the conclusion of the film we see people at the inn again dressed as medical personnel. It suggests that the young woman is in a psychiatric institution, rather than an inn.

When Christina arrives at her aunt's bedside, she is just in time to hear the woman's last words. The expiring relative urges the young woman to flee the family property. Even this dying person who lives at the feared estate is not immune to the superstitions surrounding the place.

Why such trepidation? What does it signify?

A viewing of the movie reveals that the old homestead is in fact a portal to the realm of the dead—a stairway to heaven or perhaps a gate to hell. Christina's family estate is nothing less than a symbol of Thanatos.

Auteur Jess Franco's *Christina, Princess of Eroticism* is, in a way, a loose remake of *Carnival of Souls*—a film about a young woman who is unaware of her own death.

The bell curve majority of the townsfolk fear Christina's family estate,

CHRISTINA, PRINCESS OF EROTICISM

Christina, Princess of Eroticism (1973, aka A Virgin Among the Living Dead) Christina von Blanc in *Christina, Princess of Eroticism*.

because almost everybody has a healthy fear of death. If the young woman's home is a sub-textual analog for death, then how else are we to interpret the locals' superstitions?

Despite the property's anathema status, there are a tiny handful of the townsfolk less inclined to regard the place with foreboding—just as there are those among us fretful humans who approach death more philosophically.

The sympathetic wise woman, for example, is not only unafraid of death but actively urges Christina to meet her destiny fearlessly and disregard the petty Thanato-phobic bulk of the fright-filled villagers.

Emphasizing this John "Death Be Not Proud" Donne philosophy is the fact that upon Christina's arrival home, she finds her Uncle Howard (Franco regular Howard Vernon) banging away on a piano as though nothing was wrong and there wasn't a dying person in the household.

Further reinforcement of this flippant attitude toward death is provided by cousin Carmencé (Britt Nichols), who demonstrates her disregard with hyperbolic displays of eroticism—on lurid display throughout the film—and a nod to Eros, the Freudian flip side of Thanatos.

Why are these people so unconcerned with the ultimate doom manifested by the very nature of this estate?

The dearth of fear or concern is as simple as can be: these people are already dead and have come to terms with it—for the most part.

They've crossed the veil and have been through the transition already: they are no longer worried about little things, such as death of the body.

If the understanding wise woman occupies the role of a minor oracle, then what of Linda (Anne Libert)? She is an enigmatic and apparently blind woman who also dwells on the family estate. Her physical sight may be gone but she is possessed of a higher vision and speaks cryptic messages.

She offers Christina the same reassurances as the wise woman. This oracle figure confides that Christina's soul is white. Fear is unnecessary.

To borrow traditional religious terms, Christina can take comfort because she is headed for heaven rather than speeding hell bound. If we distill this further and the meaning becomes clear: There's no reason to be afraid of death or what lies beyond.

Clues abound, though Christina is at first blind to them. She lacks the "eyes to see."

Before young Christina can even get her bags unpacked, she becomes rattled when she sees a creepy object that serves as an item of décor in her bedroom. This object is a sculpture of a decapitated head. *Christina is staring death in the face yet has no idea what is being conveyed to her.*

As with the protagonist of *Carnival of Souls,* she is clueless to the fact of her own demise, whose cause we never learn, but which is ultimately unimportant.

Another clue that death reigns over the estate is the family members' total lack of concern for the normal human need to eat.

Christina is served her meal by the saucy Carmencé on her first night home. But the woman, who is as bitchy as she is horny, warns Christina that from then on she is on her own regarding her meals.

Still later—in the dining room, no less—she stumbles upon her family "oohing" and "aahing" over a corpse's hand from which they are trying to remove the valuable jewelry on its fingers.

This crass imperviousness to the grim fact of death further demonstrates their comfort with death.

However, this scene also makes a brief comment on the covetous, materialistic mammon worship that can be a cause for tension and the fear of dying in many people. Clearly, at least some of Christina's relatives—while somewhat okay with their deadness—are still shedding their earthly materialism. Or else they are condemned to a *Twilight*

Zone sort of spiritual justice—damned to their own personal hell of lusts forever fulfilled, where carnal fulfillment is erased by infinite satiation.

A figure with little screen time but of major significance is The Queen of the Night, who lurks behind the scenes, but also appears to function as a puppeteer over the entire situation. Her presence in the film is clearly that of a supernatural personage who reigns in the shadow land of death and the beyond.

Christina is at first unaware of the presence of The Queen of the Night—as she is with so many other clues as to her fate—but she becomes aware of the spirit's presence eventually.

More clues to Christina's condition present themselves when she is told by a young man from town that there is nobody at the old estate. From his vantage point, on the living side of the veil, it is a true statement—there are no people *living* on the old estate.

They are all dead and gone.

Christina, though, is still oblivious to the reality that her presence has slipped to the other side of the veil. Her quite natural fear of death remains buried. Her obliviousness represents our human tendency to suppress all thoughts of death's inevitability.

When Christina brings the handsome lad home to prove the old estate is just another house, not a castle of doom, Uncle Howard bursts on the scene and runs the boy off. The young man does not belong here. He is one of those among the living. This is the subtext. Still, Christina hasn't put things together for herself just yet. (If only she had Bruce Willis around to guide her home.)

And then there is the old caretaker, who warns her of death hovering over the place. *Another* clue that shoots right over her head.

We have yet to speak of the family servant Basilio played by director Jess Franco himself (credited in this role as Jesus Manera). Basilio lurks in the background, mute but for grunts, taking care of whatever family or estate business needs attending. He seems an addled creature.

Could it be that the director has inserted himself here metatextually? While Franco was never afraid to appear in his own movies, the self-casting for this particular role feels a lot like Jess Franco pointing to himself as the Mad Hatter behind the scenes, steering Christina and the rest of us toward the River Styx.

Interestingly, waters of death are symbolized in this movie by a pond into which the family wanders zombie-like at the film's conclusion.

(In *Carnival of Souls*, *Christina*'s cinematic spiritual predecessor, death is a meta-presence as this film's doomed lead character literally finds her death in water. But when she crawls from the river early in the film, thinking herself still alive, the audience sees a woman being baptized into eternal death.)

Hints regarding the shadow world that Christina has unknowingly entered become more harsh and blatant after the initial clues she has been given fail to jar her into awareness.

So blithe is she to the warnings pushing at her from the subconscious (or from whatever primordial soup these messages bubble forth), that she ignores the possible danger involved in such risky behavior as skinny dipping out in the open. The risk materializes in the form of a pair of horn-dog oldsters who show up to sate their lechery by gaping at her nudity from their hideout in the bushes.

This utter lack of concern for her own welfare—ignoring the possibility of her own possible harm or death—is a symbol of Christina's complete unawareness of her true state of affairs.

Just as an attractive woman swimming nude in full view of whomever wants to watch (or do more than watch) is ignoring the threat of death, Christina is ignoring her actual death.

Things get even headier when she finds dead bats on her bed. These creatures are of course historically associated with death and evil in horror cinema. Reference the vampire film of your choice. Vampires, who often take the form of bats, are used here as symbols of living death.

Christina hasn't the time to recover from the shock of bats in her bed—and arguably in her belfry since she is too clueless to realize that she is no longer among the living—when she stumbles upon the kinky sexual antics being engaged in by her hypersexualized cousin, The Queen of the Night.

But in this scene, shock does not result from the lesbian nature of the interaction. This is a Jess Franco film; if lesbianism and strong eroticism are a shock, a heart attack awaits the viewer when exploring his filmography.

The real shock here isn't the sex (though the suggested incest is more of a startling component than mere girl-on-girl action) but the bizarre mix of death and sex. Eros and Thanatos.

The whole sight on view for Christina and the context the scene creates in its individual image components: bare raw flesh, a pair of scissors, a gash on the torso of the oracle. The overall impact is powerful.

Paul Muller in *Christina, Princess of Eroticism* (aka *A Virgin Among the Living Dead*).

The sex-mad cousin—who in another scene, wallows like a cat in heat during the funeral for Aunt Abigail—licks suggestively at the wound on the oracle's naked torso.

In a state of stark contrast to the hypersexual cousin is Christina herself, who spends so much of the film's running time undressed—be it swimming or lying draped across her bed, languid and nude, generating a thick static of sexual energy in the air—*but appears totally unaware of her own sexual nature and being.*

She is almost an innocent Lolita, completely oblivious to the things she arouses in the lower chakras of men. Why should such a strikingly beautiful creature be so unaware of the waves of sexual energy emanating from her like heat?

A possible answer is that as we age and become closer to death, we may not lose our erotic energy, but neither are we imbued with the drive of youthfulness. And the final emergence into the field of death means abandonment of physical bodies. When our biological, corporeal suit is cast off, our need for sexuality is shed with it.

The vanishing of Christina's sexual self-awareness is nothing less than an indication that, on some level, she is beginning to grasp the nature of her situation.

The corporeal life we fear to lose upon physical death is only an illusion—what Eastern mysticism refers to as *maya*.

The dilemma lies in the deceit of how reality appears to us as limited three-dimensional beings versus how reality, in its sublime full nature, truly is. Death is nothing more than a capstone on the corporeal level of existence.

A pivotal moment in the film comes when Christina's father, Ernesto Pablo Reiner (played by another Franco regular, Paul Muller), shows up for a final and critically important discussion about the nature of her existence.

He sits in an elegant chair, at a table, upon which there is a goblet. Christina sits before him at the opposite side of the table. The tableau is suggestive of a dark communion of sorts, a tenebrous Eucharist. The noose around Christina's father's neck—he died at his own hands—forms the end of a rope that disappears back into shadows, a gloomy dark into which he fades.

Outside, in the woods, her father floats smoothly backward while suspended in the air by his noose.

But she follows, nevertheless. And by going after her father, Christina is following him into the realm of death from whence he came to warn her.

The lush, melancholic music is a perfect companion to this sequence. The music is gentle and peaceful, if not particularly sanguine, and suggests at last, a realization and coming to terms with her fate for Christina.

But her transition is not yet done. A denouement of violence and dark sex is yet in store for the woman before we may quietly, reverently escort the family into its symbolic watery place of rest.

Christina follows her mysteriously suspended father—who warned her that he was manipulated into suicide by The Queen of the Night and her undead minions (Christina's family)—into a barn where his animation ceases and he returns to his still, dead state, even as Christina's family members pile into the small space and ravish her.

She awakens, back in her room, covered by a nightdress this time, rather than sleeping in the buff. It seems she is sick, with a loony-looking doctor sticking a thermometer in her mouth. It is interesting that the doctor is the same actor who appeared as one of the two voyeurs who spied on a naked, swimming Christina earlier in the picture. (The other voyeur also appears as another character in the movie.) This double casting of actors is also noted in Tim Lucas' interpretation of the film.

The assault implies a twofold meaning. On a surface level, it suggests violence and injury. Coupled with the ministrations of a doctor, a scene of dying is suggested.

Metatextually the idea is that Christina has finally effected her own death—despite her death already being a fact. By embracing the reality of her own death, she has experienced the realization of it.

The symbolism of this scene is sealed in the follow-up scene, in which Christina, nude as the day of her birth (fittingly enough) is laid out in a cross-like position amongst carefully placed candles. Religious ritual—with spiritual symbols—is suggested, despite her super-sexual cousin straddling her in a final erotic embrace.

Ritualized sex. Eros and Thanatos, once more.

The snap back to reality is striking. Christina is abruptly back at the same inn seen in the beginning of the film. Except that Christina is only with us in body, not in spirit.

We viewers are back on our side of the veil and Christina has said her last good-bye and embraced her place on the other side.

Christina, Princess of Eroticism boasts an interesting footnote.

A decade or so after the release of *Christina,* the film became the object of a bizarre re-editing and reshoot. One of the resulting consequences was the spoilerific and misleading change of title: *A Virgin Among the Living Dead.* The new title has a helluva nice ring to it, but the renaming is problematic, at best. The ghoulishly flashy but imprecise new moniker threatens to give away, even if obliquely, the undead nature of Christina's relatives.

Furthermore, the term "living dead" is heavily associated with post-Romero zombies. This titular facelift practically promises a cine-feast of flesh-eating and gut-munching splatter—which is just exactly what Franco's original movie *isn't* about!

Weirder still, the re-cut, re-shot *A Virgin Among the Living Dead* actually *is* about zombies. Director Jean Rollin, who helmed the redux version, didn't merely move extant pieces around.

Virgin, as opposed to *Christina,* is more than the rearrangement of the latter's parts: Rollin shot entirely new footage featuring zombies, even going so far as to recruit the lead actress from *Christina* to appear in the new footage.

So many of Jess Franco's films—all by themselves, without any outside "help"—are elliptical, surrealist creations. *Christina, Princess of Eroticism* is one of those films.

Rollin's after-the-fact "collaboration" with Franco's original film (and not with Franco himself), can only be described as a celluloid non-sequitur—with *A Virgin Among the Living Dead*—formerly *Christina, Princess of Eroticism*—ending up being a zombie movie after all.

THE DIABOLICAL DR. Z (1966)

Jess Franco has had truck with a significant number of different genres and subgenres throughout his colorful career. He is most known for his reputation as a creator of surrealistic, darkly themed erotica.

It may be a revelation to those with a cursory knowledge or awareness of Jess Franco's work that his non-linear concept/psychedelic pieces are far from the extent of the director's talent.

Here, at an early stage of that career, we find him tackling the mad scientist theme head-on—the mad scientist character being an especially notable fixture in the sci-fi and horror films of the 30s through the 50s. What's more, he is wrestling with the philosophical underpinnings of this classic trope.

Franco directed and also wrote (as David Kuhne) *The Diabolical Dr. Z*, one of several gothic horror films he made. Despite his reputation for psychedelic, surreal cinema, Franco was every bit as skilled at telling compelling linear stories in a gothic format.

Films like *Dr. Z*, as well as *The Sadistic Baron Von Klaus*, the Dr. Orloff films and his Dracula movies prove that Franco was as adept in this cinematic arena as he was in his more mind-bending films.

The Diabolical Dr. Z commences with what is immediately apparent as a collision course between the scientist, Dr. Z, and a man freshly escaped from prison who was to be hung that very night.

Even though the swift pacing that kicks off this gothic sci-fi affair wastes no time depositing the fatigued runaway on the doctor's doorstep, we still are not immediately sure exactly what the nature of the interaction between the doc and the runaway will be.

But then we see Dr. Z's wicked experimental device, a large platform/table upon which a patient—make that a human guinea pig— may be placed. The table has a pair of robotic arms with pincer "hands" that can be used to hold an unwilling patient in place on the table. A nasty needle through the cranium and into the brain, plus a row of ugly, cringe-inducing, spinal taps finishes this torturous tableau of science gone amok.

Post credit roll, some light begins at last to be cast on Dr. Z's diabolical motives.

He invades a convention of scientists to praise the works of the controversial Dr. Orloff. Dr. Z goes on, despite a huge room full of incredulous looks on the faces of his peers, to explain the advances that

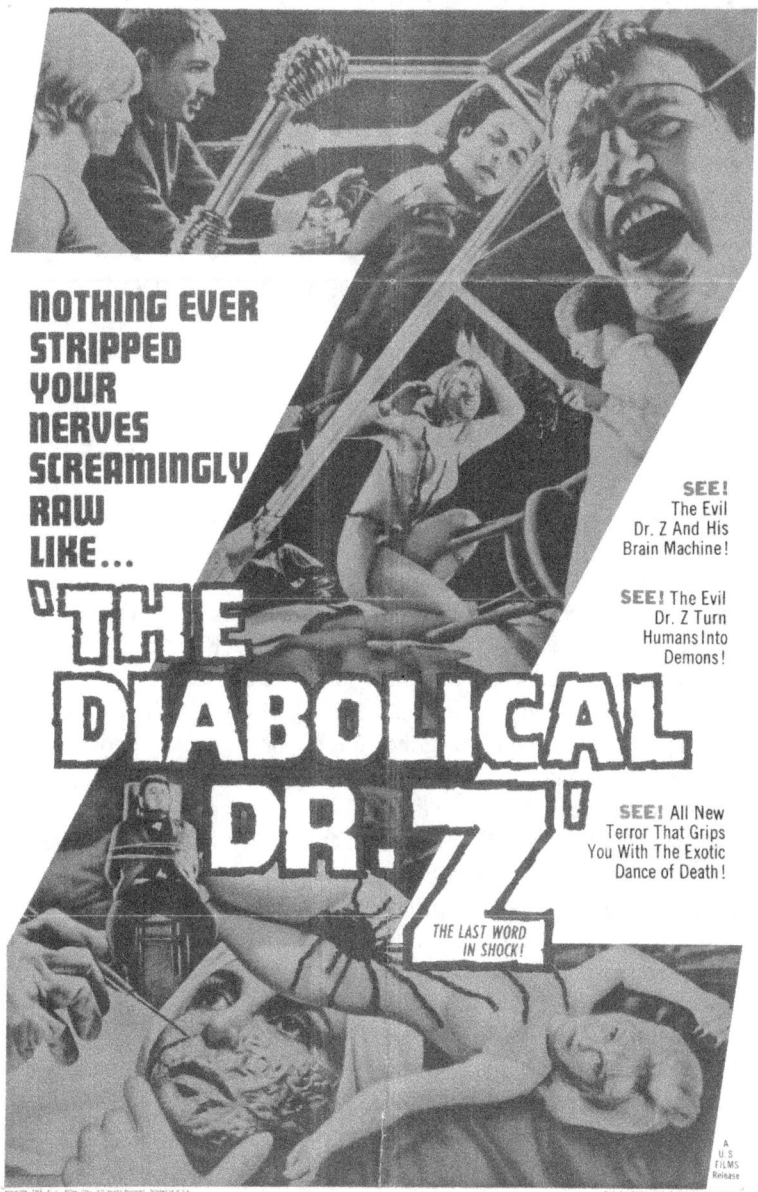

he himself has made in Orloff's theories and technology.

He claims that he is on the brink of isolating a biological source for good and evil in the nervous system of man.

This is the good news. The bad news is that animal experiments have taken him as far as he can possibly go with his research, so he now wishes to seek permission from the medical community for engaging in human experimentation.

Thus is revealed the first real inkling of what ol' Doc Z has in mind for the bad guy he has scooped up.

Another character on a collision course with Z is Miss Death, an avant-garde nightclub performer (Estella Blain), a sultry vixen whose show consists of her crawling across a person-size spider's web while acting out spidery things in sultry, erotic fashion.

Fun things like pretending to eat her prey, represented by another human form on the web with her.

Miss Death's already murderous nature, depicted early in her subplot, makes her a perfect match for the plots brewing in Dr. Z's lab.

A jump skip now to Irma Zimmer (Mabel Karr) taking over the research of her father, Dr. Z (now dead). She, rather than her father (who is really just part of a set-up), is the Dr. Z with which the film concerns itself. Irma, it turns out, is a surgeon herself and is the designer of the claw-armed device. The medical community may have driven the rogue doctor to his grave, but the next generation of Zimmer is here to keep the work going.

But it isn't a cure for the Jekyll-Hyde ills of human nature that seems to be the important goal in all this horrifying experimentation. Instead, by tapping into the good and evil centers of a person, this mad doctor is able to manipulate her victims, turning them into automaton slaves.

A bit astray from the Hippocratic Oath.

The runaway convict was certainly a welcome and useful bit of experimental fodder, but with the entrance of Miss Death onto the scene, inspiration strikes in the lab.

Miss Death, with her long poison-dipped and sharp fingernails, will be the appointed assassin to stage the executions of those medical men who, in the mind of Dr. Z's daughter, are guilty of Daddy's death.

And a showgirl with a zippy nightclub act is of course the perfect person to turn into a slave for enacting Lady Doc Z's mad mission of revenge.

Another strange facet of the experimentation is the attempt to find a

A bizarre nightclub performance in *The Diabolical Dr. Z.*

breakthrough to rid Irma Z. of her facial scarring. This is not a trope unique to Franco, nor is it the only time the director used a plot of that sort.

All this science-amok deviltry is presented with much more class than one might expect from what, in another filmmaker's hands, might be just one more mad doctor B-movie sci-horror yarn.

As it is, Franco, whose work here is considerably more linear than the ephemeral cinema for which he would go on to become infamous, delivers a lucid story laced with gothic foreboding and oddities of wrong-headed science.

The lovely black-and-white cinematography and the delicious sets employed by Franco make *The Diabolical Dr. Z* a work of real silver screen beauty.

The visuals and direction, plus the atmospheric music (including some raucous atonal jazz), are elegant packaging for what could have been ho-hum hokum. But Franco's talent elevates this film to the level of a real class production.

Drenched in mood and boasting beautiful imagery, this multi-faceted excursion into shadowy science-fiction/horror cinema is a masterpiece.

Despite the retooling of a number of ideas already present in books and other sci-fi/horror movies—even in other Franco fare—new context elevates this film with its originality and innovation.

In addition to the artful presentation of gothic buildings and spiral staircases there are other impressive visuals. Miss Death crawling on her web is not an image to ever be forgotten. Even her outfit is a marvel: a sheer, form-fitting bodysuit with a decorative spider affixed to it.

The spider's body is fitted snugly over Miss Deaths pelvic area, obscuring her genitalia, while the legs reach out across her outfit, two of the legs perfectly spread across her breasts, as though the chaste arachnid was trying to save embarrassment by trying to cover her nipples.

It's a sexy outfit and a sexy Miss Death wearing it.

Everything comes together here: lovely application of light and shadow, expert framing, a bizarre and compelling story and a score that shifts from low and mood-laced to nervous and frantic.

The Diabolical Dr. Z is not only a feather in Jess Franco's cap, it is a classic of garish (though not gory) horror, mingled with reserved but arousing erotic themes.

Philosophically, the sci-fi framework of isolating good and evil in the biological mechanism of the human nervous system is a challenge to traditional body-spirit dichotomies.

Does the attempt to locate a biological center for good and evil imply soullessness? Or can this quest point us to a holistic view of body and soul as an inseparable unit?

What does Franco seem to be suggesting—if anything? Or is he simply placing an idea in front of us to stimulate our thinking?

Whatever the case, the film is generally acknowledged to be both high quality genre filmmaking and provocative art house cinema.

Though vastly more tame than the preponderance of the director's later work, *The Diabolical Dr. Z*, with a bit of irony in tow, still effectively navigates the themes of Eros and Thanatos that prevail—along with some other ideas—throughout Franco's extensive and varied canon.

The Diabolical Dr. Z also examines conflicts in ideology.

There is the juxtaposition of orthodox science with the unorthodox and unethical, a duality pointing to philosophical considerations that penetrate deeper than just science, burrowing into universal substrata.

The thorny question of how to balance scientific advancement with the bringing of harm to living organisms is really a matter of defining parameters for the value of life.

Particularly human life.

Is life utterly sacred, always to be fought for at all costs? Or are there circumstances beyond which human life no longer takes precedence?

The Diabolical Dr. Z also touches on the clash between modes of spirituality and modes of scientific thought. A biological root of good and evil would suggest to some a reductionist philosophy in which all mental/spiritual realities are nothing more than synapses firing.

A deeper analysis of the idea, however, does no harm to spirituality, although it does indicate that the two should be in harmony with each other. A biological process associated with good and evil need not demand a reductive, materialist perspective.

It is not necessary to understand the biological component as the source of, say, love or faith; it can also be grasped as simply the biological mechanism for our experience of non-corporeal realities.

The movie makes no strict demands of us; it insists on no particular interpretation. What it does demand of us is some thoughtful pondering of the unanswered questions it introduces.

These questions are unanswered not because the film or its maker have no insight into these questions, but because the last piece of the puzzle—the answer to these intersecting, unnerving queries—is something that we must answer for ourselves.

COUNT DRACULA (1970)

Because of Jess Franco's reputation as a surrealist with a penchant for the loose adaptations of original works and non-linear storytelling, you would never expect to credit him with filming the most faithful adaptation of any novel.

Yet there he was in 1970, creating the most faithful film rendition of Bram Stoker's *Dracula* I have ever seen. Franco set out to deliver a film that followed the novel closely. Despite the telescoping of plot necessary when forging a film from a book of some length, *Count Dracula* hews closely to Stoker's novel, which has rarely been adapted with a great degree of faithfulness.

Even the original Hammer Films' *Horror of Dracula* took its share of significant liberties. Thus, despite Christopher Lee's history with the character, having already begun his career with Hammer as a Drac actor, it is in *Count Dracula* that he finally appears in a version that brings book to screen with remarkable accuracy.

While not at all intended or presented as a word-for-word adaptation (very few films can claim that), Jess Franco's *Count Dracula* is nevertheless a surprisingly faithful transition of Bram Stoker's novel *Dracula* to the screen—especially as this is a novel that has almost invariably been changed significantly in its numerous film iterations.

That is not a complaint but an observation.

I would hardly fault Hammer's *Horror of Dracula* or the film *Bram Stoker's Dracula* from director Francis Coppola.

Nevertheless, it is still quite noteworthy to discover an adaptation that not only strives for faithfulness to the source material, but also succeeds as well made cinema. Nor is it surprising to find Franco at the helm.

Any three- or four-hundred page novel is going to have to be abbreviated to become a film unless you are planning on making quite a long movie. And Franco does a surprisingly good job of condensing the story into a film of normal length.

And to declare that Jess Franco was behind one of the most literal—if not *the* most literal film interpretations of Stoker's story is something of a surprise statement to make, given that Franco is not typically known for adherence to linearity or strict adaptation of source material.

Yet here the surrealist auteur is offering us a well-paced version of the Dracula tale that, with surprising accuracy, follows the written word

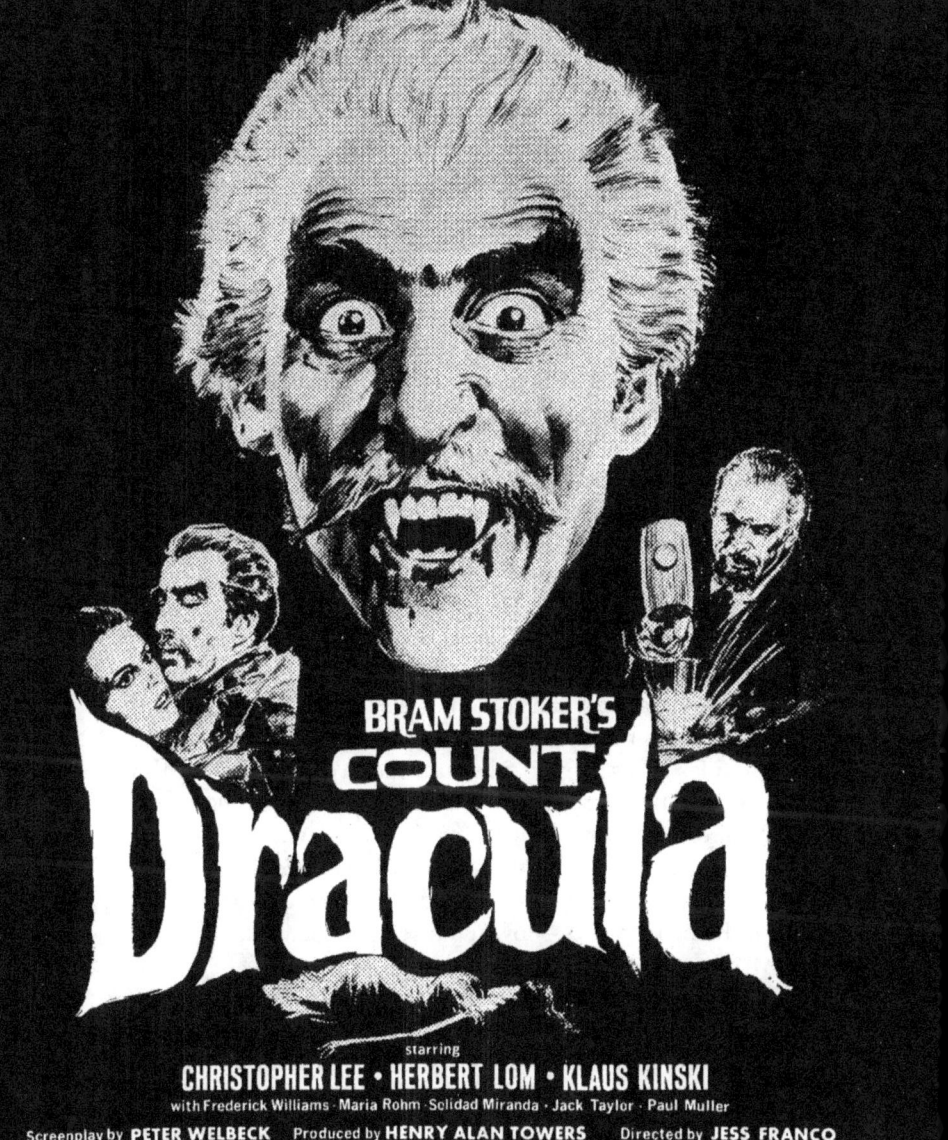

upon which it is based.

A significant portion of the credit for this achievement is due to Erich Kröhnke (story credit, as Erik Krohenke) and Augusto Finocchi (screenplay credit). Their adaptation of Stoker's novel greatly enabled Franco to create the faithful film rendition he desired.

Franco *is* a master of mood so it is no surprise at all that the viewer is plunged immediately into a place of thick atmosphere.

Indeed, how could we travel through the Borgo Pass without a prevailing aura of doom?

This director is no stranger to gothic horror, either.

So while the film's straightforward storytelling is far more in line with early Franco works, rather than the psychedelic journeys on which he would take us throughout much of his later career, the film's setting and tone are nevertheless nothing new to this versatile filmmaker.

We can be glad that he used his mesmerizing talent for mood and gothic flavors to recreate one of gothic fiction's classics and one of my personal favorites among British proto-horror fiction.

We can also be glad that he cast Christopher Lee, arguably one of the greatest performers to don Count Dracula's cape and fangs, be it in *Count Dracula* or in a Hammer flick.

In this film, we first see Lee's Dracula as the undead hoary-haired king sporting an intimidating mustache, as we do in Stoker's novel. This is a small touch, but it is a testament to Franco & Company's attempt to craft a faithful film version of the novel.

Supporting Lee in this first class production are the always-intense Klaus Kinski (as Klaus Kinsky), playing Dracula's thrall, Renfield, and Herbert Lom, as the vampire's arch nemesis, Dr. Van Helsing.

And the director's beloved muse, actress Soledad Miranda—who was to die young in a tragic accident—appears as Lucy Westenra, the central female in the *Dracula* tale. Paul Muller, who appeared in any number of Franco's movies, shows up here as Dr. Seward.

This film has a spartan air about it: the set, visual framing, a low key attitude, simple FX versus elaborate FX, etc. Its aridity accentuates the film's atmosphere and is a necessary and vital part of its design.

And a spartan cinematic approach is yet another technique with which Franco has plenty of familiarity (while also being just as comfortable with movies of a lusher variety).

There are many ways that this adaptation of Stoker's *Dracula* receives the benefit of Franco's deft touches. All the cinematic elements that work in this film are directly traceable to the various nuances of

Franco's style and skill.

In some cases the familiar Franco touch redefines itself and surprises us by showing us something we know, but is presented in a fresh light.

In other dove tailings of *Count Dracula* with facets of the director's natural style, the Franco fingerprint is classic Jess as we have come to know, love and appreciate as only Francoan art can be appreciated.

Harker's escape from Castle Dracula is one of the more hypnotic crescendos of the film's—and Franco's—style of mood-generation. The scene begins with the same relative quiet subtlety that has defined the film thus far.

Christopher Lee as *Count Dracula*.

This climactic part of the movie is far from overwrought and nowhere near as hysterical (and cinematic hysteria is another common cinema-style bedfellow of the filmmaker's). But the prevailing quietude to this point provides the contrast for the impact of Franco's sub-climax or what is basically Act One of this cineplay.

It is not until the abrupt cessation of the escape sequence—we are dropped jarringly back into *Count Dracula*'s calmer, earlier tone—that we even realize that we have been hypnotized.

So when the sudden stylish non-sequitur from build-up to relative flat line yanks us startlingly back to now, the whole small-scale escalation of the escape sequence catches up to us to be experienced all in one rush.

It really is rather startling to find Franco using quiet to amplify comparatively louder or more intense sequences—just as an artist will use empty space to create shape.

Low key has not been Franco's enduring trademark, though this style is easier to find among his earlier works. "Subtle" is not a word thrown at Franco with regularity—except maybe in this film, with my obsessive-compulsive X-ray eye piercing into symbolic substrata.

The scene that commences the mini-crescendo escape sequence is Harker's opening of Dracula's stone coffin lid and finding the vampire resting peacefully within. The scene is not overtly grotesque. We merely see black-clad, white-headed Christopher Lee laying his head against a red, velvety pillow.

But the significance, of course, arises from the context of all of that is in this story. This is how individual components of a work of art become greater than the sum of their parts: they find context with each other and a new, transcendent entity is created.

Death, and damned unlife after—a thirsty form of cannibalism—total isolation, only a devil for friend—hell with one prisoner, you!—loss of innocence, apex predator no more—fear of being bodily devoured—the loss of essence …

But ultimately, Franco's technique relies on a very simple trick of lighting. The director casts shadows that make Lee's eyes look orbless, black and bottomless and the shadows make ridges across Dracula's pale skin in just such a way as to make him appear uncanny and hideous.

No garish makeup required.

The utter simplicity of approach in Franco's version of the Stoker yarn is revelatory and refreshing. Not that I don't love his more hyperbolic work—I do, as evidenced elsewhere in this volume—but I always love to see an artist step outside himself while yet remaining true to himself.

Franco even turns toward the subtle with his knack for the sexual.

Without surprise for the initiated viewer, Franco emphasizes the erotic nature of Dracula's vampiric couplings with his female victims. *Count Dracula* unabashedly presents Dracula's ravishing of a woman as a sex act.

But Franco does so without the explicit sexual delirium much more common to the director's erotically charged works. This is yet another example of Franco applying one of his noteworthy strengths—cinema erotique—but in a refocused fashion. You are still watching Francoan erotica but in a far more subtle manner, with no effectiveness lost.

The sexual nature of the vampire's blood-draining encounters with the women upon whom he preys was present in Stoker's novel, but mostly awaiting discovery between the lines. The Eros of vampirism is pretty obvious though, no?

A fang is a small but plainly obvious phallic symbol. We see penetration by the dark masculine, as represented by Dracula, into the flesh of the woman. This penetration is a fluid exchange, although it is the male figure receiving the fluid, thus putting life into his body—not in a fetal form, of course, but as the renewed immortality of the vampire.

Vampiric penetration is a reversal, a corruption, of the natural sex act, the black mass opposite the holy union of physical love (and, implicitly, spiritual love). Vampiric encounters are unnatural; undeath walks and knows biblically the flesh of life.

It is necrophilia, but as rape, with the corpse as the aggressor—which to some extent eliminates the "philia" component, since that is where the "love of" (literally "like") comes from in "ove of death."

And rather than the living seed from the man entering the body of the woman so that it might create life—*new* life—the vampiric sex act instead draws the fluid of life unto itself.

Not the "positive" fluid of life (semen) but blood—for blood is the life!

The above line itself is an unholy recontextualizing of Jesus Christ's utterance of the same words, but with a significantly different meaning. The transfer of liquid is a negative image to that of natural coitus.

No fresh, new life is created when the male penetrates and injects his fluid life-quickening essence into the female's creative cave, the womb. Instead, the vampire sucks into himself, through his tooth-phallus, the blood that sustains the female's body.

Not only is there no new natural life created from this coupling, but a life is deleted—the woman's. And instead of a creative act of life-bringing, the stolen, transferred lifeblood is expended to sustain an unnatural life—a "life" of undeath—that already is no creation—but that which should not be.

The obvious religious components of blasphemy in the vampire mythos are not the only elements of sacrilege to be found in *Count Dracula*.

The vampiric, black-mass reversal of the pattern of divinely ordained human sex into something unholy and foul is a direct—if not explicitly religious—outrage against God, a blasphemy as clear as Gary Oldman's denouncement of God at the beginning of Coppola's *Bram Stoker's Dracula* foray.

The biological womb reflects the creative "emptiness"—the divine womb—from which all creation blossoms. Creation is definitively a divine act. As stated in *Genesis*, we are "created in the image of God."

Therefore, for Dracula to deny the creative act which would forge a new soul from God's breath (*Genesis* once again), and to do so in a way that negatively reflects the pattern of coupling established by God, is to assault the divine order.

Additionally, beyond the mere flouting of creativity, the vampiric act achieves a polar opposite extreme, leaving no doubt that this act not only neutralizes God's intent (passive refusal to obey), but also takes a defiant step to the other side of the light-dark duality.

Dracula does not stop at denying God. Dracula goes so far as to *undo*, by actively opposing, the act/will of God. This opposition is a wound in God's side through the blockage of creation. It is salt in the wound to then remove a life and further sustain the vampire's hellish existence.

Yet, *Count Dracula* is a joy to behold.

Franco veers significantly from his usual style while never betraying that style or his unique vision. And by so doing he has also made what I feel safe in proclaiming one of his finest films.

Furthermore—in keeping with the aforementioned divine order—Franco has created many masterpieces. So it is no small matter for me to declare top shelf status for *Count Dracula* in the world of Franco cinema.

It is worth mentioning that the low-key approach to the film's erotic component evident in this movie (especially given some of the other movies for which Franco is notorious) was not a decision made by Franco, but rather one made by Harry Alan Towers, the film's producer and a producer with whom Franco collaborated on a number of films.

It has been said that the (relative) chasteness of this version of Bram Stoker's *Dracula*—given the numerous erotic adventures both the character Dracula and Jess Franco have enjoyed onscreen—was onerous to Franco. He felt suffocated artistically, but Towers insisted on less explicitness.

That being said, it really is a wonder, and a credit to Franco, that even despite unpleasant restrictions, he still managed to manipulate the erotic component masterfully, however reserved, and create a film with his fingerprint that was also faithful to its literary source!

BLOODY MOON (1981)

Jess Franco was a distinctively European filmmaker and one whose works usually have "art house" written all over them, but he nevertheless left his mark on the slasher film, which I believe to be primarily an American genre.

Even so, the Franco personality is not absent from *Bloody Moon*, even if it is one of his most American films.

The film is plainly an homage to—as well as a member of—the slasher movement of the 1980s, which while inspired in part by the European *giallo*, was of itself its own genre and one dominated largely by American filmmakers. This is not to say that non-U.S. directors didn't tackle the genre, given its huge artistic and financial successes.

And *Bloody Moon*, as both homage and slasher movie, happens to be one of the better films to emerge from the early 80s slasher film movement. With Franco's direction and a solid slasher screenplay by Erich Tomek (as Rayo Casablanca), the film is a top shelf example of the early slasher movement.

That says plenty, especially since the genre is a densely populated one, with *Bloody Moon* rubbing shoulders with some truly great slasher and horror cinema achievements—*Halloween, Friday the 13th, Graduation Day, Texas Chain Saw Massacre, Don't Go In The Woods, The Mutilator, New York Ripper, The Zero Boys, Final Exam,* and more—as well as a deluge of lesser works.

References to other slasher films, overt and otherwise, are to be found everywhere in this movie. Putting on a clown's mask and use of the POV shot technique, for example, readily call to one's mind the original *Halloween*. The POV shot technique was also a classic trope of the *Friday the 13th* movies, and many other movies thereafter.

The staples of the slasher genre are entirely intact in *Bloody Moon*. Besides the already noted killer's POV shot, we are rewarded with:
- ✓ gory and creative kills
- ✓ abundant sexuality and nudity
- ✓ idiot teens
- ✓ red herrings (the whodunit slasher obviously owes a debt to the mystery genre)
- ✓ rampant partying and general hedonism
- ✓ a brooding back story complete with prologue, featuring conniving assholes

Everything you would expect from a slaughter-on-campus, body-count-driven movie!

While its European origins are not hidden, *Bloody Moon* has a distinctly American tone throughout, while never straying out of range of Franco's distinctive style.

Some Franco fans might be somewhat taken aback by the movie's comparative lack of art house flavor. But *Bloody Moon* is not that kind of movie and as stated, Franco's style is not absent or compromised. As exhibited in *Count Dracula*—in a different way for a different kind of movie—the same feat of Franco maintaining his own unique style is achieved here.

Just as sexual but less sensual.

Strict linearity.

More "mundane" material, i. e. less of a sub-textual film.

Still moody but not as ethereal.

And so on.

But when Franco stretches beyond his "standard" fare—whatever that means (you know it if you see it)—he sometimes ends up making some of his better films, as evidenced by *Bloody Moon* and *Count Dracula*.

The director captures perfectly the simplistic storytelling of slasher films, which are spun from archetypal cloth.

Consider Homer's *Odyssey* and *The Iliad*.

These classics of literature are also simple, archetypal yarn-spinning. It is too easy for thoughtless critics and persnickety casual viewers to dismiss films due to the simplicity of the story or the characters or for the lack of a complicated subtext.

Not all movies are about complex tales with complex characters and not all substrata need be nuanced or overly layered.

Don't dare to damn simplicity.

Bloody Moon is one of the movies that demonstrates Franco's versatility and his self-aware talent for rearranging his style without compromising it. This is a filmmaker who is a natural auteur.

He studied his craft one way or another, like all great artists, but the honing of his cinematic skills rode a tidal wave of instinctive, organic, innate ability.

For Franco, touching a movie makes it a Franco film.

A good example of the unmistakable Franco touch is *Zombie Lake*, a movie which he wrote, but backed out of directing. *Zombie Lake* feels more like a Jess Franco work than it does a Jean Rollin work.

Although Rollin directed the film and has a strong, one-of-a-kind style of his own, it still bleeds Franco. I would never have guessed it was a

Rollin-helmed piece had I screened it without credits and hadn't already read about the movie. Please see the Appendix for more on this fascinating film.

In *Bloody Moon*, Jess Franco adds a layer of subversion to an already subversive (for the 1980s) genre.

Slashers were sexualized movies right out of the gate and promiscuity reigned. Sex and violence combined, as part of an explicit excursion using hyperbolic examples of both, was in a prudish era a volatile combination to say the least.

Mean old ladies and unenlightened bureaucrats effected the outright legal ban of many "Video Nasties" in the UK.

Continental European movie creators were frequently compelled to shoot more than one version of their films: an explicit version and a diluted version, cut for nations with more restrictive governments.

Spanish filmmaker Paul Naschy made clothed and unclothed versions of his films, his own country being one of the nations for which the less offensive cut was designated.

This meant inconveniences like shooting scenes twice and additional expense.

A mutilated victim in *Bloody Moon*.

In Naschy's *Horror Rises from the Tomb*, one of the kills involves a topless woman getting sliced by a big, curved blade—but in the version seen by Spanish audiences (and, for the longest time, American audiences) her breasts were covered or obscured.

In the less naughty version of *Zombie Lake*, to cite an even more striking example, the opening skinny dipping scene is dipping without the skinny. Due to the method by which the sexy swimmer's scene is visually structured, the only way to clean up her act was to reshoot pretty much the whole damn scene, only with clothes kept on.

Neo-Puritanical attitudes toward the genre films developed what seemed to be a greater obsession with the phantom menace of nudity (if the boobs don't blind him, the masturbation surely will!) than with violence found in these same films. In fact, hard violence was usually accepted, sometimes depending upon the context in which it was found.

Arnold Schwarzenegger dealt out mass carnage in action flicks but Jason's antics were less tolerated.

While I do assert that I observed, if it could be quantified, a greater interest in the suppression of sexual material than in the suppression of violence, there was an unmistakable—loud-mouthed, really—frothing at the mouth—regarding violent horror. One has to wonder at the seeming correlation between the volume of 80s' reactionary anti-violence shouters and the sheer volume of gored-up ultra-bloody horror movies that popped up in Shot-On-Video (SOV) and indie scare flicks. This was also a situation that found media and pop culture still reeling from and reacting to a Vietnam War-influenced tipping point in the graphic nature of television and cinema—as well as the hard truths this more televised war showed us.

But the unholy grail of horrified parents and other concerned citizens—the ultimate antichrist of cinema sin, was—gasp!—the comingling of sex and violence.

When Wes Craven filmed the scene in *A Nightmare on Elm Street* where a sleeping female is slung up a wall and across the ceiling while slashes dealt by an invisible Freddy Kreuger appear on her partly bared torso, he was compelled to use a fake *nipple-less* torso. Why?

Because the sight of carnage *and* nipples would be crossing the line, i.e. the line between good moral people and evil filmmakers, and between getting an R rating or getting slapped with the profit-killing rating that shall not be named here.

Landing in that no-man's-land rating beyond the R—or, perhaps worse, going *unrated* (as did *Evil Dead 2*)—was a sure way to prevent the majority of theaters from carrying your movie.

At this point it seems anti-climactic, but the subtle tweak—for Franco—on the slasher genre's already hypersexual nature involves his inclusion in the film of an incestuous relationship. Even more grotesque, the brother in this brother-sister relationship has a badly scarred face.

And since we are on the subject, and because the topic of gory, creative kills cannot possibly be ignored in a discussion along these lines, there is a murder in *Bloody Moon* that in a single image epitomizes the shock of sex and violence on the screen.

One of the attractive young lovelies whose job it is to die in this movie suffers the indignity of being stabbed with a knife right through her breast, dead center in the nipple, no less. More strikingly, the blade comes *out* through her breast because she was stabbed from behind!

This scene feels as if Franco has unloaded a whole genre's worth of gloriously over-the-top mutilation in this one moment.

The blade-meets-boob shot is heady enough.

But that scene brought friends:

- ✓ a woman decapitated with a huge industrial saw (bringing a bazooka to a BB gun fight?)
- ✓ a child ruthlessly run down (this when America was still gun-shy of killing the young in movies; the film version of *Pet Sematary* had not yet popped a bunch of viewers' kid-kill cherries)
- ✓ a person losing a fight against a big, toothy bush-trimmer
- ✓ and other various and sundry brutalities.

Franco more than deserves commendation for *Bloody Moon.*

He brilliantly conjures the personality of an American slasher—tonally far different from what you think of as Franco's style—yet the movie never loses its center as a Jess Franco film.

There really is no defining the ineffable essence that marks Franco cinema, regardless of genre. All that a Francophile (as in Jess Franco fan, not a lover of France, but you already knew that) can really say is that you know it when you see it.

And that's saying quite a lot, if you think about it, considering that the filmmaker was working in a genre whose common mien is far from Francoan—other than the superficial similarities of high levels of sexuality and heaps of violence.

Because even here, Jess Franco's star still shines pretty damn brightly.

EUGÉNIE (1969)

Franco accomplished some of his best work while exploring eroticism and violence (or the murder impulse). He also earned attention on several occasions for rooting his films in the ideas of the Marquis de Sade.

The de Sade influence was certainly evident in 1969 (or 1970 depending upon one's source), with *Eugénie*, a film often tag-lined as "The Story of Her Journey into Perversion".

Franco drank deep from the well of Sadist literature and philosophy with this film. It is also, at least in some places, among the director's most erotically charged films. He fearlessly crosses the line of moral subjectivity and without hesitation hypnotizes us into witnessing the truth of ourselves.

Here we find Christopher Lee at work with Franco once more, playing the libertine Dolmance, the sort of a fellow de Sade would have most heartily approved of. One can almost hear the scratch of the marquis' quill on parchment as *Eugénie* unfolds.

Eugénie is portrayed by the succulent Marie Liljedahl. And with Harry Alan Towers producing, it is no surprise to find Maria Rohm's presence. Franco regular Paul Muller also appears.

No sooner has the movie's glow arisen than we are posthaste deposited into an ultra-ethereal film whose captivation component is immediate.

A lush but minimalist post-credits opening sequence depicts a chilling and gorgeously shot ceremony of ritual sadism that resonates like a black mass, complete with a naked female as the altar and a grim priest intoning dark incantations, offering up atmospheric chanted prayers to … well, to someone other *the One* normally receiving Sunday morning mass offerings.

A soliloquy spoken by the foreboding and frightening Dolmance introduces the themes inspired by de Sade, specifically that author's *Philosophy in the Boudoir*.

This gloomy, mood-struck introduction passes the viewer to much more mundane circumstances. At the home of a young but sexually ripe woman child, we witness her clash with a mother hell bent on keeping her sexy daughter away from corrupt influences, and we also see a father who seems detached and disinterested.

The somber mood of the opening and the subsequent bright

normalcy and its perky score make for a definite strong contrast.

And, oh, the sets Franco has uncovered for this visually stunning exercise in erotic subversion—a regular exercise for this director. The cinematography of *Eugénie* makes rich, full use of these colorful, elegant settings.

Eugénie is a movie that represents the vast difference between erotic art and pornography. And the loving, thoughtful visuals are part of that indefinable essence that separates art house from whorehouse.

Eugénie is a languorous piece of cinema, content to float—albeit not rudderless—along the eddies of its own ethereal current.

The poor titular young lovely hasn't a clue that she is facing a journey into white slavery that has nothing to do with overly horny Middle Eastern sheiks. Her own dad is selling her to a man-and-wife team of extreme libertines.

Eugénie is on the teetering brink of not only losing her sexual innocence—which is hanging on by a thread, anyway—but losing it in a jarring, delirious fashion.

The subtext scratching at the surface here involves the shock-and-awe trauma that sexual awakening is for some of us.

It can be emotionally devastating, and Eugénie's shattering

introduction to sexuality is no weak fumble in the back of a car but instead, like the scalding immersion in hot water suffered by the lobster bound for a plate, she is slammed into a depraved world where pleasure is pain, and awkward teen boys and failed orgasms are the least of a young woman's concerns.

And since we are on the subject of sex, let us double back and connect that arousing theme to the aforementioned cinematography. I mentioned, and rightfully so, that *Eugénie* is laden with potent visuals. But there is naturally more to the glorious sights than well-decorated old buildings or beautiful seascapes or landscapes.

Franco inserts "landscapes" of stunning women into this movie and the loving way in which he creates their scenes of erotic encounters—be they gentle, caressing connections between two female friends or the sadistic abuse inflicted by Christopher Lee's diabolical character—illustrates another way that movies like this stand apart, a separate kind of creature than those flicks that are flat exercises in soft core prurience.

Once the kidnapping has been effected, the film slips from the ethereal into a consuming, hallucinatory mode that allows Franco, among other things, to show off his use of color, shadow and visual imagery.

It is truly amazing how Franco can bring out such lushness in his visuals using deceptively simple minimalist techniques.

This is an experiential film whose second half is practically an extended dreamlike sequence and works on your mind like swinging a watch in front of your face and counting down.

The erotica is so *charged*, it is as if a powerful bolt of static electricity could zap out of the TV and penetrate your brain and gut. With this dizzying, mind-bending psychedelia, Franco smoothly elicits waves of atmospheric energy from a sublime joint effort, a whole transcendent life evolved from a woven tapestry of:

- ✓ the director's uber-artful eye
- ✓ the fluid, deliberate sensuality that changes direction sharply enough to jar your teeth
- ✓ the galvanizing, more frantic sadism that emerges from that abrupt shift
- ✓ the aural hypnosis induced by the edgy psychedelic music that fills all the cracks of space in this multi-layered cinematic fabric.

And then we are unceremoniously dumped back into a tone of lightness and frivolity that is equally jarring in the reverse direction. (Meanwhile, Lee's narration of the philosophy of enlightened sadism returns sporadically, at key points perfectly punctuating the film's flow.) There really aren't any adequate words to describe Franco's kaleidoscopic madness—a madness of genius. The man throws you face first into a manic orgy of sadistic gluttony—fresh from supple tenderness—and not only do you find yourself disturbed viscerally, you also find yourself supercharged in your belly, your sexual chakra glowing like a ruby.

I could have said "it creeps you out but also turns you on", and while that is technically correct, that assessment is far too reductive for such a luminous experience.

Visceral disturbance is one of several powerful experiences to be had in *Eugénie*, which is really one big powerhouse of an experience. No John Holmes opus could ever compare to the pure, unadulterated, psychosexuality and erotic spirituality of Jess Franco working at the top of his game.

Eugénie's dramatic escalation strongly parallels the progress of de Sade's *120 Days of Sodom*, which starts with the merely filthy or perverse and then increases in intensity step by step to the murderous and violent.

In a like manner, this Franco flick begins with light transgression (bisexuality, girl-on-girl), then increasing the intensity of transgression by (friendly) orgy, finally hitting a sudden drop-off into razor-sharp and inebriating sadism.

All this reaches a surprising (or not) culmination, the tipping point breakthrough, when dear Eugénie's own sado-murderous inner demon awakens.

Lee's character spared not the rod that he might not spoil the child. He led Eugénie through a gauntlet of depraved pain so that she could be a phoenix reborn from the ashes of her own suffering into the sadist angel of the ubermensch.

This, dare I say, is a divine arc. This is eroticism and sadism manifest as religious experience.

Harry Alan Towers, who was responsible for the strikingly muted sexuality in Franco's *Count Dracula* package, was obviously not, as this film proves, always committed to asserting a stranglehold on the filmmaker's erotic art sensibilities.

For as much as Franco felt that his hands were tied during his Christopher Lee sojourn into Dracula country, there is no evidence of creative stifling in *Eugénie*, a film that ranks very high in the pantheon of the director's best work.

DRACULA, PRISONER OF FRANKENSTEIN (1972)

Jess Franco's versatility and scope allowed him to apply his love for eroticized horror not only to movies like *Eugénie*, but also to what the aforementioned Tim Lucas refers to as Franco's "monster rally" pictures.

Essentially, these films paid homage to the classic silver screen monsters, but were interpreted and re-represented through the one-of-a-kind sight of the visionary Franco.

There is Al Adamson's *Dracula vs. Frankenstein*—and then there is Jess Franco's *Dracula vs. Frankenstein*. Known in the United States as *Dracula, Prisoner of Frankenstein*, the film's onscreen title is *Dracula Contra Frankenstein* ("Dracula Against Frankenstein").

This movie—and its sister film of the same year, *The Erotic Rites of Frankenstein*—are clearly odes of love to those old school horror movie monsters. These monsters have been visited over and over again in cinema; I am sure Universal's vintage bugbears were a major influence on these movies.

Notably, Hammer Films did several Frankenstein and Dracula pictures from both monster franchises. Some of these feature Christopher Lee and/or Peter Cushing. Hammer also did their own versions of the Wolfman and the Mummy. In no sane universe could Franco withhold his own vision of some of these creatures.

Of course, *Dracula, Prisoner of Frankenstein* and *The Erotic Rites of Frankenstein* are not Franco's only forays into such material. In an earlier chapter in this volume you will find my ode to *Count Dracula*, Franco's shockingly faithful adaptation of Bram Stoker's classic work of British gothic fiction, *Dracula*.

The director's *Daughter of Dracula*, inspired by J. Sheridan LeFanu's vintage lesbian bloodsucker tale, "Carmilla", is examined later within these pages.

This visit into Dracula territory starts right off with Franco's notable prowess for minimalist Gothic cinema. The foreboding mood steps in and wraps its cloak around you immediately—not that you will put up any fight. Franco's love for the gothic monster classics is already on full view.

While the director may in many circles be more known for his psychedelic erotica—including erotic horror—he has also repeatedly proven his superb mastery of the quiet gothic.

Gonzo Franco may be, but that is not all he is. And even in what for him are subtle films, his signature style bleeds through. I think it is actually rather amazing that such a maestro of cinematic frenzy and subversion is able to in effect, detune his considerable flair and not lose his unmistakable presence.

An acting analog to this scenario would be Robert de Niro, whose presence is typically nothing short of screen-filling. He is, however, able to magically subdue his dominating mien in his portrayal of a loser in Quentin Tarantino's *Jackie Brown*. He allows Samuel L. Jackson, also a formidable screen presence, to overpower him in every scene. Robert de Niro makes a brilliant artistic choice in doing so.

Just how could a director like Jess Franco resist a monster mash? Universal sure couldn't and a cinematic horror mash-up certainly seems to be right down one of Franco's several bizarre alleys.

The first major plot point, which starts a domino effect that brings together several key gothic horror figures from classic literature, is the kidnapping of Dracula (Franco regular Howard Vernon). This scheme is orchestrated by none other than *Dr. Frankenstein*, played by another of the director's regulars, Dennis Price.

A stake is pounded—for safety's sake, you understand—into Dracula, who promptly and conveniently turns into a bat. Harmless—for the nonce—and reduced to portable size, Dracula is taken into custody.

Of course, Dr. Frankenstein would not plan any mad scientist shenanigans without his beloved creation along for the ride, so it's only a matter of time before this stitched together golem of flesh is on the warpath.

And where would history's greatest vampire be without some luscious vampirettes mucking about being all sexy and looking for something to suck on?

(I realize we have had this discussion elsewhere already but, come on, vampires are inherently sexual creatures, both as characters and as mythic symbols. You are going see this stuff come up again and again—pretty much any time you sink your teeth into a Jess Franco vampire movie.)

Just for good measure, as though lycanthrope enthusiast Paul Naschy has wandered on to the set for no good reason, there's even a werewolf thrown into this marvelous mix-and-match cult gem. Naschy is another European filmmaker with an enormous fondness for the old creature features and monster mashes, as witnessed by his string of werewolf movies.

There is a peculiar flavor that comes from mixing ultra-classic horror styles and characters with Franco's edgy style. The overpowering atmosphere is not only dripping with vintage gothic horror, but it is also shot through with that indefinable Franco flavor.

And leave it to the director to give us a melodramatic, brooding dish of gonzo gothic that kicks you in the ass by booting you *sans* warning into the middle of a bawdy nightclub where a vaudevillian vixen is singing to a crowd of adoring males (and a few women, too).

I am assuming this nightclub is at least a few miles from the castle where Dr. Frankenstein is busy waking up his beast, since everybody is all happy and cheery and, I'm guessing, safely enjoying themselves in town.

Except ... even in town, it isn't safe. (Isn't that how angry villagers with torches and pitchforks and stuff typically end up chasing a monster in the middle of the night—because the evil somehow trickles down into their lives?)

No sooner does the singing, sultry, sexy performer make it up to her dressing room than she is snatched by Frankenstein's monster, who carts her off posthaste.

Next thing you know, she is laid up on the Doc's metal table. Looks like she has moved on from burlesque to the more important role of helping to further scientific experimentation—however villainous said experimentation may be.

In part, the experiment appears to involve drowning a poor bat in blood. And, really, it actually looks like that is what Franco may have done, but I cannot verify if the bat was real or not.

Of course, we know that Frankenstein is employing his technique for restoring Dracula from his stake-rendered suspended animation. I suppose. A literal blood bath does seem an ideal way to soak some life—or undeath—back into the old boy, right?

What exactly the singer/dancer was needed for is not immediately clear, but just keep watching.

Franco doesn't waste any time putting together all the ingredients of this mondo monster *ghoul*ash (forgive me ...).

This is a saucy little movie that is more about combining all of these beloved monsters and madmen into a fever dream of film, than it is about conveying an overly specific, detailed story.

Not that this film is one of Franco's numerous non-linear surrealist endeavors; in this case the filmmaker hews more closely to a traditional plotline than in his numerous more ecstatic efforts.

But the whole point is that the director is ready and willing to take you on a crazy ride if you are willing to go with him on this wild journey.

Make that a wild trip minus the LSD.

Do you need the science manual from Doc Frank's laboratory? Or do you just need some terrific monstrous mayhem from one of cinema's great auteurs?

I think you know the answer to that, and if you do not, then either (a) you are reading the wrong book, or (b) you have come to the right place for an introductory baptism into Francoland.

By which I mean this book you are holding.

As cool as it is, though, *Dracula, Prisoner of Frankenstein*, might not be the ideal cinematic introduction to Jess Franco's cinema.

Although this movie is representative of one field of Franco's film endeavors—an overlap of two, really, if you consider gothic horror and monster movies to be separate subsets of the filmmaker's canon—I don't think this film is necessarily the ideal representative or epitome of either the man's gothics or his monster movies (or his combinations thereof).

However, to play devil's advocate against myself, I will say that the movie is probably more accessible to newbies than some of his other works.

But to put a wrap on this rambling tangent, I daresay no single film can be considered typical of the director. His versatility illuminates a broad spectrum, while still operating under the broad umbrella of Franco's inimitable style.

I suppose if you are far more disposed toward one kind of movie versus another, you could use that as a starting point for deciding where to begin exploring Franco's world of movies. That is pretty much what I did.

I began by consuming Franco from the horror side of his canon. That still meant devouring some erotica along the way, but I have no objection to that as such.

At the time I had yet to develop a mature taste for purely erotic cinema (in this case, I mean erotica versus erotic horror or erotic sci-fi or whatever). But erotic cinema grew on me, especially as I couldn't work through Franco's horror material without also encountering his devilish and uniquely stylish approach to cinematic sensuality and sexiness.

So if you prefer, say, gothic and/or monster pics, you will likely land a lot closer with this movie than you would with something like *99 Women* or *Sadomania*. When you decide to take the Franco plunge.

I think the psychosexual erotic subversion of *Eugénie, the Story of Her Journey Into Perversion* was my real tipping point. As is clear from my chapter on that film, this film gripped me like no erotica ever had. After that, I'm not sure there was any turning back.

Franco's *Dracula Contra Frankenstein* is a true original. The film's only derivative quality, if it may be so called, is its simple use of the vintage horror movie icons from yesteryear.

Beyond that, all the staples of monster moviemaking are completely turned to the service of Franco, who, even on his worst day, makes nothing mundane or usual. "Usual" is not a word that even belongs anywhere in this book except for putting a "not" between "Franco" and "usual."

Unless, of course, I was to speak of Franco's "usual" type of movie, which would be an oxymoronic statement, and which would make me an idiot.

The one exception would be if I was trying to make a VERY broad statement, and using the idea of a ... ahem ... "usual" Franco film strictly as a term of convenience. Sorry, but I'm making that exception to give myself an out in case I have talked of "usual" Jess Franco movies somewhere else in this book, and I don't remember doing it. I really don't want to be an idiot. Really.

Dracula, Prisoner of Frankenstein may not be one of Franco's overtly psychedelic films, but it is nevertheless a masterwork of dense but fluid mood. And the film does stand out among its fellows in the Franco canon—his other Dracula and Frankenstein pictures.

I do not mean the movie stands out as superior, but simply that it is its own creature—if you'll pardon me the pun—and has its own personality.

This film is distinct from the others (who are each distinct in their own right), and that includes its closest relative, *The Erotic Rites of Frankenstein*.

VAMPYROS LESBOS (1971)

For several reasons, *Vampyros Lesbos* sits at the pinnacle of the Franco work that explores the crossroads of extreme erotica and pure head trip. The soundtrack alone is enough reason to sink into the luxurious offerings of *Vampyros Lesbos*. The film is something of a "Carmilla"-inspired gender-shift adaptation of *Dracula* while also being 100 percent a creation of master craftsman Jess Franco.

Vampyros Lesbos is one of the more experiential films in the director's canon, which is saying quite a lot. The bizarre and funky music and sleek erotic vampirism that fill the viewer's psyche nearly from beginning distinguish this film as a singular experience, even, a little bit, from among other top Franco efforts.

This is also one of the most memorable and noteworthy Franco forays featuring Franco's original muse Soledad Miranda, who plays the central character Countess Nadine Carody, seductive vampiress.

Miranda died young and tragically and left Franco emotionally destitute until he found solace and new life in the inspiration of Lina Romay. Thankfully, however, Fate decreed that the alluring Franco-Miranda pairing that is *Vamyros Lesbos* would come to be.

She is happily joined by actors and Franco film frequenters Dennis Price (as Dr. Alwin Seward) and Paul Muller, who performs as Dr. Steiner.

From its initial frame, *Vampyros Lesbos* puts you into a realm of pure psychedelia. Make that PSYCHOdelia.

There is a crazy soundtrack of lush electric organ and strange vocal mutterings, plus some stringed instrumentation that sounds like it came from India or at least from a Beatles album when they were fully doused in their tubs of LSD.

And that's the crescendo score for a tableau of succulent lesbian vampire sensuality.

The film is shot with spellbinding color saturation that practically induces a hallucinogenic experience without the use of chemicals.

A surprise pullback revealing that this is a nightclub performance robs you of nothing. It isn't cheap. (Although the movie does have you thinking it must be a real-bloodsuckers-in-plain-sight kind of deal—like Lestat the rock star.)

And the audience is bathed in supple color-and-shadow, too—a magnificently realized sequence!

A couple watching the show is quite impressed and the wife's dreams are soon beset by powerful Sapphic and vampiric visions that lead her to orgasm again and again.

She is disturbed—but also intrigued and quite thoroughly aroused.

These are such theoretically shocking things for a woman who thought herself straight—both the lesbianism, and (for anybody, you would think) the vamipiric aspects.

What could repulse (the woman-on-woman sensuality) and horrify (the vampire aspect)—instead work as a strange and compelling lure upon the woman, drawing her toward forbidden sensuality.

This is such a supple, tinglingly erotic, and gorgeously artful film.

One can barely begin to watch *Vampyros Lesbos* without immediately wondering if this movie doesn't deserve a permanent place in the top echelon of Franco's films.

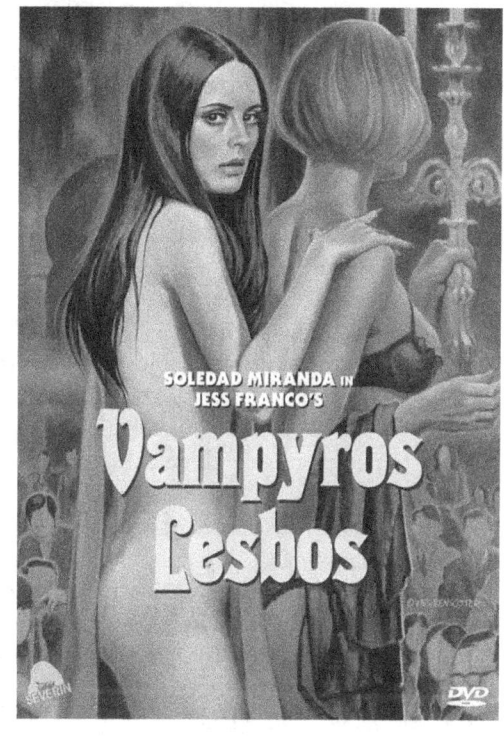

Vampyros Lesbos is an absorbingly rich experience, as it assaults you psychedelically with an array of acidy music and a plethora of alluring images.

Director Jess Franco's cinematography is in absolutely top form here.

And his fetish for quirky scores is realized by a peak musical performance.

This movie is such an immersive experience, I find myself momentarily at a loss for words, if such an absurdity is to be believed.

Vampyros Lesbos takes a dazzling look at one of Franco's favorite cinematic and philosophical themes—that of the innocent drawn into new worlds of erotic experience, worlds forever on the fringe of everyday existence.

Be it vampirism and lesbianism, as it is here, or forbidden forays into S & M, as evidenced in many other Franco movies, this is a filmmaker who likes to explore erotic awakenings and escapes from innocence.

I say "escapes" because we are not dealing with mere sexual awakening.

Rather we are confronted with the awakening of a person into higher realms of moral cognition. We see flowerings of the ubermensch in female form, the realization of realms beyond the mundane world of the unenlightened, a liberation from herd-thought.

We witness the heady intake of rarified air by someone emerging from their chrysalis into a bold, new and awakened form.

Again, the vampire emerges as a symbol of transgressive sexuality.

It is amazing how Franco amplifies (what in earlier popular iterations of vampirism) was merely subtext.

Franco is not pulling this eroticism out of his ass. He is graphically highlighting the substance that already lies just beneath the surface of the vampire mythos.

Franco is elucidating—he is enlightening us as to the true, visceral, sensual nature of the vampire.

And he is doing so with a manic vision all his own.

By drawing us into a haze of erotic delirium with captivating music, some of his finest visuals, stimulating performances and more, Franco is really tapping into something dark and delicious that resides at the heart of all of us. And by showing us "evil" as pleasurable, he challenges moral convention, as is his wont.

This film is among the high points of the director's cinematic subversion. It is easy to see why Franco was considered by the Roman Catholic Church to be "the world's most dangerous filmmaker".

The alarm expressed by the Church tells me that he has struck a deep chord and that it was a chord that was badly in need of striking.

Those of us who have fallen in love with Franco's work also feel the striking of that chord, but for us it is not a threat.

His films are frequently challenging, but Franco's art is transcendent. There is something angelic about it in an enlightened, devilish way.

It is as if he is subverting what everybody assumes to be the truth to show us actually what the truth is.

He is coaxing us to throw out useless moral paradigms and to join him in a special place of liberty.

"Come," be beckons, "and discover that the things they told you to be afraid of are nothing of which to be afraid."

Franco was a brilliant cinematic artist, and doubtlessly one of the world's most unique. I feel more than comfortable saying that, even though there are plenty of unique filmmakers out there.

No one does erotica like Jess Franco does.

VAMPYROS LESBOS

Soledad Miranda in *Vampyros Lesbos*.

Nobody does Sapphic love the way he does.

Nobody approaches vampires the way this visionary does. One need not look beyond *Vampyros Lesbos*.

But once one has seen this film, one must surely crave more—and there is plenty more. Franco has repeatedly demonstrated a fondness for all things erotic, for lesbian affections and for vampires, be it the Count himself or his sexually quickened descendants.

I find it interesting that the seduced wife in this film still takes some pleasure with her husband, even after the profound sexual awakening that has grabbed hold of her.

What this situation suggests to me is (a) that she has discovered a heart of bisexuality in herself, and/or (b) that she is still transitioning. If (b), this signifies that she is Lot's wife looking back, though maybe not with the longing that turned Lot's wife into a salt statue, but rather with a bittersweet yearning that is saying good-bye, rather than clinging desperately to that which she has known.

Take it as you will.

Soledad Miranda in *Vampyros Lesbos*.

Regardless, this is a movie about transitions. Life-changing transitions.

Paradigm shifts.

Epiphanic knowledge that after knowing one may not un-know.

These are permanent changes in what one perceives to be one's self.

Vampyros Lesbos is a film about initiation, about being led by a mentor who has already crossed the point of no return into an orgasmically scary new level of understanding.

The immortal seductress in this case is a sort of erotic bodhisattva leading this young woman away from her world of the mundane and into a world of spiritual awakening through the flesh.

(In a certain way, Franco and Clive Barker's tenebrous visions of flesh and spirit, pain and pleasure, dovetail with each other, though each visionary has his own quite distinctive approach to exploring such material.)

The seduced heroine of this picture suffers trepidation and fear even as she is born into this new, heightened reality. But every change is scary until we make it through to the other side.

There is a parallel here to the mystic understanding of letting go. It is part of the enlightenment process.

This is what Christ—speaking in more basic, down-to-earth terms, referred to when he spoke to his followers about the impossibility of a loyalty divided between service to spirituality and a single-minded worship and pursuit of Mammon.

The more attached to this life a person is, the harder it is for them to attain spiritual advancement.

And yet, Franco revels in pleasure.

Which flips us over to the other side of this peculiar coin of paradox.

Spirituality involves release from attachment, and yet what fools would we be to insult God by failing to enjoy this realm of existence and the pleasures he has placed here for us. The trick is finding a middle path, as Buddha said.

Franco, with his deceitfully complex films, wrangles with this dilemma, touching on it in a way more real and profound than could be achieved by any discussion that must be hamstrung by the limitations of words.

Plot-wise, there is a strong resemblance between the overall arc of *Vampyros Lesbos* and the Stoker novel *Dracula*. But this resemblance is more than merely "*Dracula* as a lesbian."

Vampyros Lesbos is, in part, the essence of the story contained in the Welshman's book, but re-presented as Franco's own personal vision.

Nobody but Franco could mix sex and death in such strikingly beautiful ways.

Sex is only bad, the filmmaker could be telling us, if you think it is. Death is only fearful if that is how you see it.

Jess Franco is a cinematic ubermensch, for certain. And the subjects he speaks to us about in his movies are those subjects that threaten the excessively conservative or tradition-restrained religious establishments.

They offer God, through their channels.

Franco's art is a direct challenge.

Vampyros Lesbos preaches a sublime yet psychedelic gospel of self-understanding and provides direct third-eye access to the formless divine.

99 WOMEN (1969)

Those of us who can be counted as fierce aficionados of so-called "exploitation" cinema—although many of these movies should actually be classified as art house cinema, this film included—might be inclined to take the Women In Prison (WIP) genre for granted.

How wrong we would be.

The WIP film as we know it owes a great and terrible debt to Jess Franco. His *99 Women* is a pioneering effort in this genre. This film is yet another of Franco's collaborations with writer/producer Harry Alan Towers, who again proves himself more than the relatively prudish movie maven that his muted vision of *Count Dracula* might have suggested he was.

The very fact that this is one of the first modern WIP movies, a film that—with Franco's finesse—helped set the standard for these movies, demonstrates that Towers was quite open to rich mixes of sex and sadism.

The auteuristic production and ideasmanship executed by the savvy Franco, reveal a man who has risen to the top ranks of bold European art house cinema.

This seminal WIP project features the great Herbert Lom and, unsurprisingly, Towers' significant other Maria Rohm as Marie, the newest inmate at the prison.

In the final year of the 60s, there arose from the mind of Jess Franco the film *99 Women*, a pioneering movie in the Women In Prison genre, and one of the pillars in the wild and woolly world of WIP cinema. Franco doesn't give you any illusions that you are in for a nice ride. These are not 99 women ready to unleash your primal porno fantasies.

These are 99 women in a women's prison run by a cruel bitch of a prison superintendent, a character that helps define the archetype for the kind of character that Dianne Thorne (in Franco's own *Ilsa the Wicked Warden*) and Mary Woronov would become known for.

The opening shot is one of grotesque beauty—sticks piled around a dead animal being assailed by flies. This is a warning shot, and as soon as that stunningly framed visual has settled in, some of the titular 99 women arrive at the prison island and we get our first view of the evil superintendent.

In a striking juxtaposition of ideas, we see this evil woman a few minutes later standing atop a prison parapet (this is, as a character warns early on, the "Castle of Death"), staring contemplatively across the sea with a dandelion stuck in her mouth.

What a shot and a work of art all in itself.

As usual, Franco is busy making things beautiful with his keen eye and his trusty camera, regardless of how dark the object of his beauty-seeking lens actually may be.

The warden of the prison is a uniformed man (Lom) with a taste for elegance. We meet him in his swank surroundings, sitting at a table before a simple but classy spread of tasty food.

He issues a warning to the superintendent about an inmate who died recently in her "care." (This is why there are but 99 women, counting the new girl, rather than an even 100.)

The poor abused-to-death inmate showed marks—the superintendent really must be more careful. This is a quick indication that the warden, while perhaps not *as* proactively or physically cruel as the superintendent (he seems more aloof and doesn't immediately broadcast a mien of overt cruelty), is not the nicest of people.

To create more of the contrast with which Franco imbues the film, we observe the warden offer a bit of food to his pet bird. A big man, he is

unconcerned about the murder of an inmate, but worried about optics and propriety, feeding his delicate avian friend. This makes for quite a striking image.

The superintendent's cruelty is further revealed by her utter lack of concern for an ailing inmate, whose physical suffering is (in the view of the superintendent) the inmate's own fault—the inmate's insolent and rebellious attitude, you see, has earned her repeated (and justifiable) punishment.

The prison doctor is concerned, but the mean old heifer makes it abundantly clear that *she* is overseeing the *punishment* of these women. That is why they are here, after all. Rehabilitation doesn't have a hell of a lot to do with it.

The new girl—"Number 99"—makes her first big mistake (not counting getting herself stuck in this prison to begin with) when she calls the superintendent over to the cell regarding her concern for a suffering fellow female inmate whose wounds are causing her much pain.

The vicious superintendent, rather than summoning immediate medical help (the doc shows up the next day, apparently), threatens the newbie with a long stint in the punishment cell for being insubordinate.

Apparently, seeking help for a fellow inmate is insubordinate behavior.

Of course, we know—and see for ourselves, soon enough—that the warden himself is also cruel, even if his cruelty is not about taking a direct delight in fiendish punishment.

His meanness is in part passive—he allows abuse to happen as long as a proper façade is presented to any higher authorities who may come snooping around.

He is also a lech and not above using the women for his own prurient enjoyment: he declares how hot it is and tells a couple of inmates to make themselves comfortable.

Seems what he really wants is his own live lesbian sex show.

We see that his cruelty is less about the overt enjoyment of inflicting misery on the women under his charge and more about the greedy satisfaction of his ruthless desires. Ironically, this has the unfortunate side effect of inflicting pain and mental anguish on the inmates he uses for his pleasure.

Cruelty is still the end result.

The callous and lustful warden gets his live sex act after one of the women tries to balk, but the other one—more knowledgeable in the ways of survival at ol' Castle Death—catfights her, slapping her ass back to bed where suddenly things turn "tender"—for lack of a better word.

Perhaps "gentle" is more to the point.

Gentle on the surface, given that the inmate initiated into sex shows for daddy warden is doubly coerced, not only by the warden's horny authority but also by the more experienced inmate who is not about to allow the other woman to "fuck shit up" for her in this already screwed-up situation.

99 Women is a study in cruelty, a cinematic Stanford Experiment that gives us an ugly autopsy of the human soul, revealing the demons that live in all of us.

The superintendent enjoys her power and she has so much of it that she is able to enjoy it to nearly unbounded sadistic extremes. The warden has the soul of a rapist and is happy to turn his lusts to the helpless women.

And the women prisoners, reduced to a less human and more animalistic life, can be quick to turn their ferocity on each other.

But a new development, unwelcomed by the superintendent and warden, at least, changes the dynamics. A woman inspector, of equally strong mettle as the ogress in charge, arrives at the Castle of Death; she is has been sent by the prison authorities and has arrived to observe what is suspected by prison authorities to be a corrupt operation.

The superintendent knows damn well they are looking to oust her and is none too pleased, but what can she do about it?

This inspector wastes no time in offending the superintendent by displaying a compassion motivated demand to examine the new girl, who has been banished to solitary confinement. This trip to solitary features the added attraction of being chained to a wall at just such a height as to prevent the inmate from ever getting comfortable.

The prison authority watchdog insists upon the prisoner's removal to a different cell and even has the audacity to ask the prisoner's name. At this, the superintendent screeches that the prisoners have no names—only numbers!

Given the kind of movie this is, we have every right to expect some erotica, but much of it is delivered in scenarios which most of us would consider ugly. Still, the erotica is not all of the vicious variety.

During an inmate's flashback, for example, we are treated to one of Jess Franco's lovely and visually captivating tableaus of feminine erotic expression. Even a WIP movie can have beautiful moments and of course Franco has made one of this moment.

The flashback offers us the insight that these women in prison—some of them, at least—come from already wretched backgrounds. The aforementioned erotic segment is embedded in a back story that is scandalous and not just a cloud nine of sensual pleasantries.

Franco is astounding in his capability to show us both the tenderness and ethereal beauty of sex, but also its claws. This talent is part and parcel of his talent in fusing transgressive and often disturbing sex with death and violence, all the while creating works of beauty with these combinations.

The elegance of the living quarters enjoyed by the superintendent and the warden provide a bold contrast to the lowly conditions endured by the prisoners, further reinforcing the awful nature of their existence upon our awareness.

Franco's *99 Women* also features the loss of innocence motif one finds over and over in the director's films—not that these ladies came straight from the full bloom of uninitiated maidenhood into the horrors of the worst in prison life.

But to be involved in dark sexual dealings outside prison in the free world is a far different situation than being thrust into hardcore imprisonment with no escape from the boldest of cruelties.

So we have an essentially good-hearted woman—Prisoner 99—as the pivotal figure of the film's events, a person thrust deeper into a travesty that she could never have imagined before arriving at the Castle of Death.

Some of these women *are* victims. The situations that landed them in jail included forces outside their own control. They are the victims of circumstance as well as the victims of a bloody, cruel system of incarceration.

The excessive brutality of some of the female guards also hints at another subtext of *99 Women*. Their behavior illustrates the viciousness women can have toward each other.

Martian men and Venusian women and all that, but there is some truth to it all. Men can become raging mad and beat the hell out of each other, but women can be capable of a particularly keen viciousness and competitiveness, especially toward each other.

I know a teacher who said she had no problem breaking up fights with men, but she would never again (after getting slammed into lockers) try to break up a fight between two women.

The not-nice female guards also lead us back to the Stanford Experiment. Perhaps not all of these guards were cruel (except potentially) before securing their prison positions, but the seductive lure of power over another human being carefully nurtured the potential for evil hidden in their hearts and has unleashed their latent cruelty.

This film is also about despair. In fact, at one point the prison authority inspector asks the superintendent if, after all the time she has worked at this prison, she has ever felt the sense of hopelessness there.

The final act of the film involves an escape attempt. And while there is no Steve "Papillon" McQueen about, there is a truly tender moment of straight sex between an on-the-run inmate and a man who is helping the escaping women. In its way, this moment represents a return to normalcy and freedom as much as the escape itself does.

Franco is not suggesting that there is something wrong about lesbian sex, or homosexual union in general, but when someone is forced into acting against their nature, it doesn't matter what the against-their-nature act is—it is still a violation and a visceral trauma.

There is a provocative irony in this film that "normal" heterosexuality is emerges as a deviant sexuality here.

99 Women is certainly not about the superficial aspects of sexuality, although that layer of sexual understanding is there; the film is more deeply concerned about the imprisonment of one's own soul. The violation of something as innately a part of the self as one's sexual orientation can readily represent the larger idea of the violation of the human spirit itself.

Although sexuality is a deeply embedded component of one's humanity, the soul is a significantly more profound part of that humanity.

LUST FOR FRANKENSTEIN (1998)

Late in his career, Franco abandoned film and turned to shot-on-video projects. For some—even for many, maybe—this was a travesty and a major downturn in his career.

Then why does *Lust for Frankenstein* persist in my mind as a noteworthy film in the Franco canon? Because fan-boyish fear of change blinds some to the fact that as different as this movie may be tonally—video has a very different feel to it than does film—*Lust for Frankenstein* is also an example of pure Jess Franco, a Franco deep in his element.

Here is a director who was always devising creative methods for shooting cheaply. Despite budget constraints, Franco still managed to produce great films, all the time continuing to experiment with his art. Shooting on video was a supremely natural direction in which to expand for Franco.

Video may possess a whole other feel than does celluloid—perhaps a more raw one—but it is wrong-headed to assume that using this format will result in an inherently inferior product.

In 1998's *Lust for Frankenstein*, Franco cast both his second great muse Lina Romay and the younger, contemporary adult film star Michelle Bauer, an actress who has worked extensively in Alternative Cinema.

Romay stars as Moira Frankenstein, the latest generation of *those* Frankensteins. Bauer appears as "Goddess - The Creature."

Clearly, Franco is playing in one his favorite territories and paying a revisionist visit to classic monster cinema.

Lust for Frankenstein is the curious tale of Moira Frankenstein, daughter of a bodybuilder—and no, I don't mean a weight lifter.

Her deceased father appears to her in bloody visions and demands that she take up his work. Clearly the inclination to play Mr. Potato Head with dead body parts runs in the family.

In other words: "Dear daughter, I need you to pick up where I left off, performing abominations against nature and bringing to life some inhuman beast made from human bits. Cool beans?"

So what this amounts to—broadly speaking—is that we are simultaneously immersed in classic Franco material and post-modern Franco material.

On one hand, this is Franco in classic form, as just noted, performing

an homage to even more classic horror with his return to the Frankenstein myth. But this is also Franco in the new realm of indie cinema, one that has replaced the drive-in and the grindhouse as a venue for what mainstream theaters won't show you.

The era of home video releases for underground moviemaking meant another artistic evolution for Franco.

His style remains and permeates, as a knowing Franco fan would anticipate, but there is also a shift in that style. Embracing a new medium of filmmaking cannot help but put a twist in your style, especially if you are Jess Franco, a director addicted to filmmaking and singular self-expression.

But the twist is not unwelcome. I like seeing Franco find a new mode to explore with his perennial style.

In case you are wondering—though you really shouldn't have to ask these questions—the director's penchant for jazzy scores and strong erotica remains. This is still entirely Franco land, which means sex and mood-inducing music, bizarre horror, and violence.

Franco is one of those battery bunnies that just kept going and going. I believe only death stopped this relentless purveyor of subversive art.

The video format provided him some new techniques for fiddling with the look of things and made for some sexy sequences with gonzo visual presentations.

Some will see all this as "cheap", but those who believe so come from a particular crowd of video naysayers: their arguments may thus be dismissed out of hand since these naysayers can so easily and artlessly dismiss—out of hand—a challenging approach to video cinema made by a master.

Lust for Frankenstein is as compelling in its own distinctive way as earlier, more "traditional" works, traditional by Franco standards, that is … if this is not a relatively meaningless statement.

Even fans of old-school Franco might be inclined to regard this movie as too campy, but to me it is more gonzo than plain camp, if I may be allowed the distinction. Although obviously hyperbolic in nature, *Lust for Frankenstein* may perhaps be qualified as a particularly rarified and sublime expression of camp.

At any rate, as I have argued during many cinematic debates, camp is too easily disregarded by most critics as a silly or stupid, etc. form. This may be true in regard to low camp that occurs unintentionally with a work that was meant to be "serious" but ends up otherwise.

But there is also a higher, intentional form of camp. Consider the 1966 *Batman* TV series or even Joel Schumacher's *Batman & Robin*, which is a wonderful but universally misunderstood movie. To paraphrase Pee Wee Herman: "They meant to do that."

Franco may be beyond most people's cinematic understanding—his work by its nature bucks conventional cinematic narrative and thus alienates mainstream-only viewers—but that does not negate the truth of his art.

In *Lust for Frankenstein*, we see the sort of tweak we have every right to expect from Franco: when Moira Frankenstein's creation first appears, it has boobs! We are dealing with a she-monster! Of course, this isn't exactly a Francoan innovation since such a concept was pivotal in the original *Frankenstein* novel.

However, to depict the monster as attaining strength by supping on blood is an innovation and to have her running around full-blown nekkid and exuding some lesbian tendencies ... well, that seems a bit more of a Franco touch, doesn't it?

Of the latter-day Franco movies I have seen from this final era of SOV filmmaking, *Lust for Frankenstein* is certainly among the best. The movie is creepy and even a little weird despite what we have come to expect from the director. Some of this is due to the video medium, which does require a bit of an overhaul in atmosphere, but using the video medium does not interfere with Franco's self-expression.

Of course, this is another argument in favor of SOV as a brave new medium for Franco, rather than a bad idea and a downgrade in the quality of his cinematic art. Video offered the dynamic director yet another fresh avenue to pursue his one-of-a-kind art.

A hint of lesbian tendencies goes beyond hint and becomes all-out lesbian enthusiasm.

After the creature saves Moira from a would-be rapist (whom Ms. Frankenstein subsequently uses in her experimentation to energize the she-monster further, if I interpret the scene aright), the two engage in an energetic sexual romp.

Despite being a stitched-together lover is not in fashion this season (nor was it in 1998), this is a peculiarly arousing sequence. One suspects that its very subversive nature is what makes the scene unusually erotic.

After all, if you and I like Jess Franco movies, then we must surely have a little deviant in us somewhere, yes?

Of course, Franco explores a number of his favored themes:
✓ sexual violence
✓ transgressive eroticism
✓ the heady mix of Eros and Thanatos
✓ defiant cinematic narrative structures
✓ slippage between reality and the hallucinatory
✓ stylish cinematography.

One of the more compellingly bizarre sequences in *Lust for Frankenstein* is that of the she-monster pleasuring herself while watching a shirtless stud split wood. The axe-wielder hasn't the foggiest notion that he is being watched and is performing in a one-man live erotic show.

When Moira discovers the creature doing this, the monster invites her to join in, whereupon Moira approaches her from behind. While thrusting her hips against her creation's backside, Moira's hands are wrapped around her front, assisting the stitched-together bundle of unrestrained sexuality to achieve her pleasure!

It is a curiously male position that Moira has assumed here and the visual is very much mimicry of straight sex, with a male thrusting his organ into his female lover from behind.

Is this scene simply a clever device to visually stimulate the viewer with a little cognitive dissonance? Or is Franco suggesting the internal sexual complexity of the bisexuality spectrum?

The creature is plainly turned on by masculinity, but also, by the nature of her already depicted lesbian side, she asks Moira, a woman, to physically join her for the bodily pleasuring.

There is a table-turning here. The stereotype is that women are the objects of voyeurism and sexual objectification, while in this film you have a pair of women sexually objectifying a man. The axe is also a super-aggressive phallic symbol. This tool is not only a rod, but one with a deadly and sharp tip. Plus, the axe creates a cleft in wood, and the penis enters the cleft between a woman's thighs.

Another scene that grabs the viewer is one in which the she-monster attacks someone and Moira chastises her violently with a cruel lashing. In some ways, this incarnation of the Frankenstein creature is the coalescence of Franco's overarching Eros-and-Thanatos duality.

The creature is a sexual being, but also a thing of horror, stitched together from the parts of others. And her ravenous sexual urges rival her proclivity for violence. She is a symbol of the grotesque as well as beautiful.

Eventually, in a poignant symbol of the she-creature's self-awareness (analogous to having a soul), she begs Moira to end her life and provides Moira with the key for doing so.

It is said that even if human beings were immortal, they would eventually reach the point that they desire death. Just as we see the creature's life of aggressive hedonism culminate in a desire for death, our pleasure in life (which brings with it its opposite—pain, or lack of pleasure) may eventually transform itself into a weariness for life.

OASIS OF THE ZOMBIES (1983)

I have been under the impression that *Oasis of the Zombies* is generally among the less beloved, shall we say, of Franco's films, at least among his more well-known films, at any rate.

But you want to know something? This is one of only a handful of zombie movies I own. This isn't Franco at his most artful or most subtle/subtextual or most psychedelic or most erotic. This is pure Franco horror filmmaking (sort of—more later), although the movie is not without his talented, distinctive imprint.

Franco has done many different categories of movies and straight horror is actually not the most common sub-genre to pop up in his work. Erotic horror, sure, but just straight horror? I can't think of too many examples.

But this movie is one of them. Part of what makes 1983's *Oasis of the Zombies* so effective is something you can't throw a rock at without hitting in a Franco film—mood, mood, mood! *Oasis of the Zombies* is stacked and loaded with atmosphere.

Additionally, the movie is conceptually more original than quite a number of zombie films. Plus, the zombies are among the coolest-looking walking dead I have ever seen, even without the benefit of high-tech Hollywood effects.

And although the beginning proves to be a pretty classic horror movie set-up—drawing very broad parallels to other horror films—the credits have not even arrived yet when Franco presents one of his nice cinematic touches.

A couple of young hottie types are out for fun in the desert ... for whatever reason. They find a nice oasis and decide to check it out. Things get super weird super quick.

What kind of desert oasis has old guns and Nazi military vehicles lying around? Worse, this oasis also has old *Nazis* lying around ... underground. They may be dead, but unfortunately they are *undead*.

One of my favorite shots from the movie has zombie arms shoot up, intersecting each other at a roughly perpendicular angle—like an X made from crossed zombie arms—to grab both ankles of one of the poor girls.

This scene creates a striking image, simple but terribly effective, and a fantastic example of Franco's directorial eye.

Following the credits we discover ourselves in ... a treasure hunting

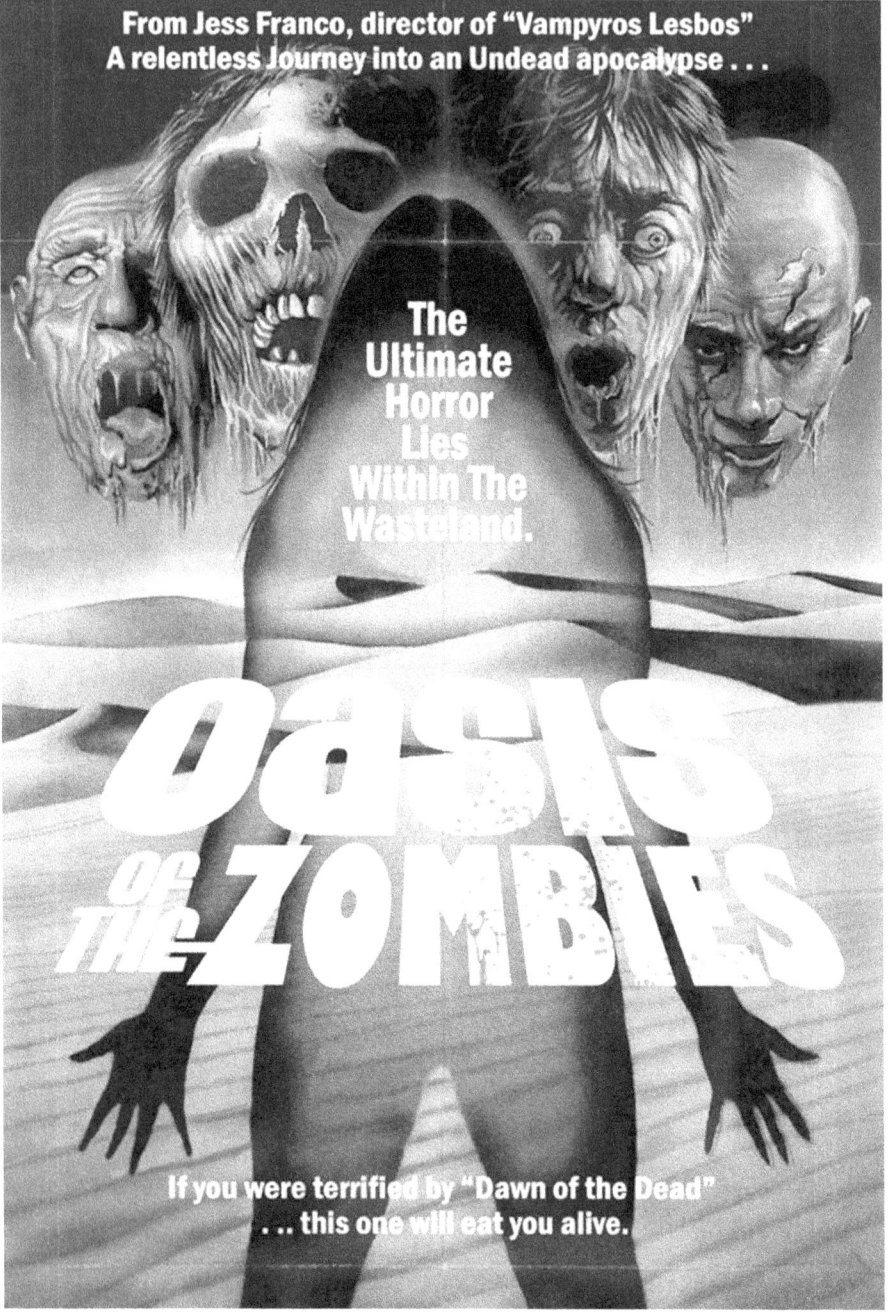

movie? Yes, we do. I told you it was pure horror ... "sort of."

Here we have one of the more interesting and rather unique bits in Franco's *Oasis of the Zombies*. This is an old-fashioned get-to-the-treasure first plot that leads its characters into a Nazi zombie movie ... set in the desert!

Once the treasure map is introduced it is promptly and violently stolen.

This has barely taken place when a group of young people are drawn into the intrigue. Here we have your traditional batch of young folks on a collision course with horror movie stuff, but in a most unconventional horror movie.

Oasis of the Zombies blends zombies, teen horror, treasure hunting, and war cinema.

Just because a movie has Nazi zombies running amok does not mean it is even remotely a war film. But while this is not a war film, per se, it is *partially* a war film, which a lot of Nazi zombie movies can't really claim.

As with *Zombie Lake*, scripted by Franco and directed by Jean Rollin a scant few years before *Oasis of the Zombies* (see the Appendix), the director found an organic way to insert war flashbacks into a walking dead picture.

And yet, these two movies, even with the odd dovetailing of both dead Nazis *and* war movie style flashbacks, are quite distinct from each other—despite the fact that both movies were written by Franco.

Oasis is possessed of a cinematic personality that sets it apart, if not necessarily above, its zombie movie peers. The mood and uncommon plot, together with Franco's one-of-a-kind auteurism, combine to create an underrated yet must-see zombie picture.

It is also a little bit of a thrill to see both fun B-movie machine gun action sequences appearing alongside grim undead doings in the same film. And leave it to Franco to put together that sort of gourmet platter for his freaky fans and fans of the freaky.

There is also a fantastic big multiple-zombie attack around thirty minutes into the movie's running time after the treasure-seekers arrive at the oasis.

The gold-guarding undead get pissed-off enough at these encroachments on their nice little corner of the Middle Eastern desert to emerge from the sand in numbers and start racking up a body count.

The scene is spooky and the grisly low-tech zombie make-up remains remarkably effective.

The Middle Eastern setting itself (wherever Franco actually shot it) is worth mentioning for its own merits. We have a colorful, exotic backdrop to the proceedings that a lot of zombie films cannot claim. Or a lot of horror movies, generally, I reckon.

For contrast (because we know Franco digs contrast) there is an attractive scene where the young folks are walking along the sidewalk back in town with Muslim prayers piping out of speakers and loyal Muslims are kneeling on the ground along the sidewalk. The kids casually walk around them. The kids are not Muslims and they are not expected to participate in the five-times-a-day prayers as long as they do not interfere. The scene is not important to the plot, but provides a really nice touch that adds even more texture to the film.

And just as this scene stands in contrast to the zombie attacks and the war movie flashbacks, it also contains its own contrast in terms of the vast difference between the somber, reverential mien of the worshippers and the casual, but not disrespectful, attitude of the young westerners out for a stroll.

The Eastern style music that dominates the soundtrack also enhances the flavorings that help make this a one-of-a-kind zombie flick and makes it one of my favorites within the genre.

EXORCISM (1975)

One might expect that a film from this director with this title, and at such a time, would be Jess Franco's answer to William Friedkin's *The Exorcist*. But, believe it or not, it is anything but.

Rather, it is a film about obsession, lust masquerading as faith, murder hiding behind holiness. We see an inversion of sacred and profane concepts that characters of traditional morality would condemn as transgressive, but are themselves the victims of real evil in the guise of holiness.

Franco himself stars in *Exorcism*, playing one of his best roles as a defrocked Roman Catholic priest who is apparently too fire and brimstone for the traditional morality crowd. Casting himself as an ex-priest is one example of the satire and dark humor Franco has on tap for us in this movie.

This ex-priest character further expands Franco's love for irony when we learn that his vastly different current profession is not only secular, but is that of a writer of occult stories. We see that his new profession also represents an inner clash for the former priest.

It is this conflict of the soul that stands at the crux of *Exorcism*. When the collarless holy man discovers something early in the film's running time, confusion becomes a dropping of the floodgates for the man's spiritual confusion and repressed self-righteous anger.

Long-time Franco collaborator Lina Romay appears as Anne, one of the females unlucky enough to be close to this movie's events.

This one is a doozy.

We open with a black table displaying knives and a live dove. The camera sure does like that dove. Doesn't bode at all well for the dove.

Nor are things looking too terribly bright for the woman, completely naked but for leather knee-high boots and bound upright against some wooden contraption. Sure enough, flogging and scratching—by another woman wearing barely more clothing—commence. We knew torture was coming. Welcome to *Exorcism*.

This grotesque opening comes with a twist, its surprise being that the torture ritual is actually a show at an avant-garde nightclub/dinner theater establishment.

This is, of course, a storytelling tactic that Franco enjoyed and used more than once in different movie contexts, *Vampyros Lesbos* being only one example.

The introductory scene is atmospheric enough to raise goose bumps and capture your attention.

The components of this sequence unify to make it a heady piece of cinema all by itself:
- ✓ the slaughter of what appears to be a real dove (a quick decapitation, for what it's worth)
- ✓ the smearing of the bird's blood on the freshly punished nude-in-boots chick
- ✓ a group of spectators as cool as a cucumbers at a dinner theater
- ✓ an array of bizarre and beautiful onscreen images
- ✓ that dark and groovy ultra-lush organ score

This weirdo show (all the more engaging for being weirdo) starts out on the disturbing note of showing woman-on-woman torture. But the stage act climaxes with sex-loving woman-on-woman erotica with Upjohn's Sex Spectrum gauge needle pointing way over in the S&M portion of that hot and heady sexual spectrum.

Then the scene reverts to the grisly and ends in the dominatrix figure stabbing the bound woman in the belly with a dagger, a scene pregnant with phallic subtext.

Even though the sequence does reveal itself to be part of an avant-garde dinner theater performance, these moments of film are among Franco's darker depictions of the Thanatos/Eros yin-yang.

The sets are arguably among the best Franco has chosen for the shooting of his movies. They perfectly match the atmosphere the director is constructing here. The mood is intense and thick in *Exorcism*, and the sets are one of the elements that make this film such an effective piece of erotic gothic horror.

And not at all unusual for Franco, he jumps you into more nightclub scenery, a little trick he seems to enjoy. One of his artistic patterns is the juxtaposition between otherworldly horror and/or erotica and the world of the mundane, be it city streets or rockin' nightclubs. And a regular old nightclub provides a strong juxtaposition with the avant-garde theater that presented the grim opening black mass scenario.

Thematically, we have Franco's ever-present interest in "normalcy" versus "deviancy."

Exorcism also boasts one of Franco's more interesting horror plots. In his central role of the ex-priest who now writes lurid tales, Franco's character discovers the existence of the "black mass." But he is unaware that it is staged for entertainment, and is not a genuine act of

Left Hand Path religious devotion.

Somehow he comes to the ridiculous conclusion that he has been witness to a bona fide black mass. His misunderstanding of this event acts as a dangerous trigger, a catalyst commencing in a one-man crusade worthy of the gusto displayed by Islam-battling Roman Catholic knights.

The writer-priest is obviously one of Franco's juxtapositions of dark and light, sacred and profane, or whatever yin-yang you prefer to describe this dichotomy. The character was once a priest—a symbol of virtue and good. Now he writes—i.e. creates from his own dark mind the dark things that hide in its shadows.

His pen, rather than inspiring people by composing spiritual homilies, instead titillates them with tales of the occult and satanic. This is of course the polar opposite, conceptually, to what he once did when he followed a religious calling.

The women who act out the wicked, sacrificial mass also enjoy moments of sincere sensual tenderness off-stage, revealing that their private lives are a marked contrast to their public lives.

The erotic encounters seen in their show are charged with blatant images of death and violence comingled with sexuality, but their real relationship behind-the-scenes exhibits the Eros minus the Thanatos, providing another layer in Franco's matrix of dualisms.

There is a truly disturbing sexual urge behind the ex-priest's oh-so-ardent pursuit of purging evil from this pair of pretty but devil-smitten (as the loony ex-priest sees it) women.

Even while his religious zeal waxes strong, an almost rapist-level degree of domination wells up in him, with both urges merging into a single action that combines the killing urge with the sexual urge.

In yet another obvious aligning of sex and death, Franco's ex-priest has demanded the undressing of one of the women, upon whom he stretches himself.

He places his hands around her throat and interrogates her about the black mass. Then he shoves a cross in her face, demanding that she kiss it, repent and confess that she is possessed. It is hard to miss the analogy to overzealous religion and its forceful, often damaging ways.

The sequence continues with the ex-priest gouging her with a knife, though not fatally, presenting a very phallic image and quite a strong visual allegory for rape. He chants some kind of prayer in Latin over her before chaining her, standing, to a mirror.

The chanting continues. This is a morbidly gorgeous sequence and one of the most compelling in Jess Franco's canon. And it is in this scene that we discover just why the former priest is a former priest. This is where we learn that Franco's character was too severe for the Roman Catholic Church.

I am guessing that the ex-priest wishes that the Inquisition hadn't gone out of fashion several centuries ago.

Exorcism is, partly, a study of obsession and how religious zeal is still zeal, and zeal can be blind and deadly. However religious the motivation underlying uber-idealistic zeal, zeal can still prove to be as evil as that which it seeks to combat. And all too often, the pursued "evil" isn't evil at all, leaving that status entirely to the "true believer."

Here then is a story in which the black mass isn't actually evil and its conductors are the innocents, while the self-appointed representative of the Roman Church (as the body of God on earth and defender of that which is holy) is the villain. And, oh, what a villain he is!

A rogue ex-priest applying diabolical techniques toward the repression of what he perceives as evil!

This movie shares a spiritual understanding of the philosophy of Satanism *à la* Anton LaVey, who objected mightily to the Christian hypocrisy of proclaiming prudishness in the name of God, all the while hiding its sins.

LaVey, who as a youth was hired to play the organ for both carnivals and tent meetings, was angry when he saw people carousing "sinfully" at carnivals only to show up at the tent gatherings and play church.

He also despised what he saw as a church that, with false morality, demanded the suppression of people's natural, healthy desires.

Franco, while not as strident as LaVey, nevertheless forges a contrast between actual good perceived as evil and real evil in the guise of good.

As if to punctuate all this, there is a beautifully shot orgy sequence in the middle of *Exorcism* that is a cinematic sight to behold. This scene is not only powerful because of the exceedingly generous display of lovely, young flesh, but also because of Franco's powerful execution of the scene.

Franco knows how to create cutting edge art that will take what some see as the basest of human desires, film them in a transcendent way so that they manage to get under your skin. He connects with the viewer both carnally and spiritually.

DAUGHTER OF DRACULA (1972)

Jess Franco made a number of monster movies in 1972, among them this one. And while this movie wasn't as much of a passion project as other '72 Franco monster mashers (treated elsewhere herein), this film still stands up as a superior slice of Franco mayhem.

Daughter of Dracula reveals the filmmaker as a re-creator of vintage movie creatures, a master of erotic cinema, and an expert in subtlety, pulling off—right in front of you—linearity-breaking narrative jaunts in what seems an otherwise orderly (by Franco standards) forward-moving story.

This movie also features Franco's penchant for re-using locations in new contexts. If you've seen *Christina, Princess of Eroticism*, you will recognize a set or two, presented in fresh fashion for his story. (In point of fact, this movie was made about a year before *Christina*.)

Daughter of Dracula also boasts a pair of actresses Franco would go on to use again in the brilliant *Christina*.

One is Britt Nichols, who appears as Luisa Karlstein, doomed to suffer the vampiric curse of the Karlsteins. This family name is a connecting thread throughout these loosely connected horror pictures, including the *The Erotic Rites of Frankenstein* and *Dracula, Prisoner of Frankenstein*, creature features (also from 1972) discussed elsewhere in this book. An Irina Karlstein appears as the lead character in the director's ethereal masterpiece *Female Vampire* (1975).

The other actress appearing in *Daughter of Dracula* is Anne Libert, who plays Karine, a vanilla housewife who falls under the sway of the vampiress.

Daughter of Dracula is a take on J. Sheridan LeFanu's female vampire short story "Carmilla." A brief opening narration connects Franco's vision of "Carmilla" with the Dracula legend. He does so by placing the film's gothic horror action at Karlstein Castle where once, we are told, dwelt Count Dracula.

Then, *sans* delay, we are transported from ancient lore to modern fright.

Handheld camerawork offers the POV perspective of a stalker prowling an attractive woman's apartment as she undresses. The visuals are accompanied by some quiet but mood-imbued jazz scoring and provide a terribly unsettling opening after the quick intro voiceover.

It is a suspenseful scene, and unnerving.

In *Daughter of Dracula*, a woman uncovers her unholy connection to a count who was a vampire, thanks to a revelation provided by an old, sickly loved one. She receives a key that sets her on a journey into the blood-and-sex world of vampirism.

Strange gets even stranger when the corpse of a naked woman is found on the beach, apparently washed up from the ocean. Peculiar, indeed. The viewer is drawn into the suspense of wondering how these story threads are going to merge.

Here, in this film, we discover another solid example of Jess Franco's singular filmmaking talent as he is able to create beauty from minimalist, spartan materials. I have developed an affection and admiration for his ability to make so much from seemingly mundane materials.

Franco knows how to use aridity in his aesthetic favor, and he knows how to find good locations for settings (used once or more!) and to use them to their fullest potential. Visual potency, as always, is a hallmark of the filmmaker's entrancing works.

Core actors appear and re-appear. Franco has even been known to recycle footage shot for one movie and use it another, so that sometimes even the actors must have been surely surprised at appearing in a film that they did not actually act in).

Some might criticize the director for reusing sets he has previously employed, but this would be an unfair criticism. There are major recurrent themes in the man's work whose realization is greatly enhanced by these sets. And I am only noticing the particularly distinctive ones, so there are probably additional sets whose reuse I haven't noticed.

(On a tangential note, Michael Bay reused at least one snippet of film twice—albeit in one case it was dramatically altered with the computer generated imagery (CGI) superimposition of, I believe, a transformer. The footage was originally used in, as I recall, *The Island*.)

But recycling is fascinating technique, especially as it is atypical of most cinematic productions (not counting various, unrelated pictures using the same famous landmarks, etc.). And since Franco is atypical of cinema-makers, then, well, you know …

Franco's passion for nightclub settings is also evident. I've noted that even the shots of a crowd in a club or of an audience in some shadowy dinner theater are all masterfully lit and shot.

Franco endeavors to put a degree of beauty in every frame of his pictures. This director has a singular sense of beauty, as is showcased by his impressive canon.

That canon contains more than 150 films, I believe, and I recall reading that even Franco himself was not sure how many films he had made. And the subject is further complicated by the existence of numerous alternate versions.

Most of those alternate versions were not, I suspect, at Franco's instigation or with his collaboration.

In fact, the ones with which I am most familiar and spring most quickly to mind, are the alternate versions of his more graphic films, in which the more offensive segments have been excised or trimmed for

Britt Nichols in *Daughter of Dracula*.

release in less tolerant nations—such as the U.S., for example.

Daughter of Dracula is one of Franco's quieter films, which is worth mentioning, considering how the swelled delirium of a Jess Franco experience can peak in one of his more psychedelic pieces.

An extended sequence of pretty eroticism unfolds while a man plays soothing piano music atop loving images of female flesh coupled tenderly with female flesh.

That this is a vampiric encounter does not detract from the charm or sense of soft sensuality that pervades the scene.

The vampiric bite looks like it stings more than just a little, but it also looks exotic and one cannot help but get the sense that the one being penetrated, while instinctively squirming against the hurt, is also desirous to a significant degree of the transgressive, painfully keen pleasure she receives from the teeth of her lesbian lover.

I've said it a gazillion times already in this book, I'm sure, but I can't let this sequence pass us by without commenting on how, yet again, we discover a powerful piece of cinema presenting in shining form Franco's expert ability to merge (with no visible stitches) the seemingly contrary forces of sex and death into a transcendent unifying whole.

In other words, we witness a new level of creation—and arising from the ashes of Eros and Thanatos—the participants sacrifice themselves in the name of the sublime to join in union as a new entity that is both—and perhaps neither.

Franco was a profound artist, even if a majority of cinephiles and moviegoers in general lack the perception to see.

Franco is not for everybody.

His works are parables, not to enlighten the uninitiated, but as sultry feasts for those awakened to the luminescence of outsider artistry—or for those with potential and on the brink of awareness, those who need only the right piece of creative endeavor to nudge them irreversibly outside the mainstream.

(I feel compelled to make the disclaimer that I do not have anything against mainstream art—I enjoy plenty of it—but I do believe that adhering to only that which feeds the ticket-buying bell curve and disregarding deeper dimensions that may be explored for the cinematically brave tends to leave a person shy of some wonderful and enlightening cinematic experiences. The same is naturally true of any medium of art.)

Daughter of Dracula is a surprisingly contemplative movie, which adds some distinction to it within Franco's canon.

Not that his other movies aren't just as thoughtful, but often the thoughtfulness is the quiet Tao in the midst of:
- ✓ the orgasmic turmoil of hyped-up, skittering jazz scores or brooding organs
- ✓ mesmerizing and ultra eye-popping film visuals
- ✓ challenging juxtapositions that simultaneously create and dissolve cognitive dissonances
- ✓ the beautiful gonzo brilliance of a director who is like no other.

Franco is never short of surprises to pull from his bag of versatility tricks. *Daughter of Dracula* is one of his more sedate movies and it works all the more for its quiet sensuality.

TENDER FLESH (1997)

Here we have another Franco movie that was shot on video, the format to which he switched during the last period of his movie-crafting life. This film is a Franco reworking of *The Most Dangerous Game*, a story core he has visited before (see *Countess Perverse*).

The Most Dangerous Game, from a Richard Connell short story, was first filmed in 1932. The director approaches this classic literary (and cinematic) tale of a wealthy sociopath whose wild game hunting thrills have run dry. Faced with a fading interest in life, he turns to a new novelty—hunting the most deadly prey of all.

Humans.

Returning to work with Franco in this adventure of literal man hunting is his beloved Lina Romay.

The picture opens immediately to the revelation of a colorful visual palette from the director and this palette includes some savory young nubile female flesh. A sexy, young, aspiring actress is looking for a job and she finds one that promises her a gig and some fun. At first the job is plenty of fun, sexually pleasurable, a hedonist's Eden. But she learns too late that when the fun ends for her, it is just getting geared up for her hosts.

They like to hunt game of a particularly peculiar nature.

Before we get to the terrible island of doom, Franco's *Tender Flesh* opens with an extended sequence of erotic and rather kinky on-stage performances. The viewer is treated to a bizarre tableau of curious erotica, ethereally presented and hypnotic.

This is, after all, one of the things at which director Jess Franco excels. The gonzo imagery is stranger than strange and involves, at one point, a gorgeous dancer wrapped in what appears to be a long strip of leather bound around her delectable nakedness. She is between two big, non-realist male figures, each with enormous phalluses, which the dancer caresses while smoky jazz music plays.

The viewer has *definitely* found himself or herself deep inside the searing cinema that thrives majestically in Jess Franco territory. The eroticism is thick in this movie, starting off drenched in pheromones and the sexual energy is kept high throughout. Franco is fully charged here.

The island is gorgeous, but of course our unaware victim will all-too-soon forget all about tropical paradise. First she will be distracted by steamy erotic encounters way beyond the norm, then she will be way beyond distracted when she has to run and fight for her life. All orgasmic joys are in the past tense.

Franco has—shocker!—added some potent S&M components to his interpretation of *The Most Dangerous Game*. Imagine, for example, the family dog under the table begging for scraps. Now, change a couple of details. It is not the family dog, but a human female. And she isn't begging for scraps; rather, she is delivering sexual pleasure to the people seated at the dining table.

The scene is outrageous—but also subtle. While some pretty out-there S&M stuff is going on under the table, Franco allows us to derive some of our vicarious pleasure comes by seeing the above the table reactions of those being pleasured.

This is a pretty intense scene, even for Franco. It is a fusion, surprising in its subtlety and yet an outlandish expression of onscreen sexuality. And conceptually this is some pretty crazy stuff, even by comparison to some of the filmmaker's other psychosexual set pieces.

It is such a rare, divine joy to see a director practically outdo himself or at the very least, witness a filmmaker of this bent and artistic magnitude treading on the boundary of an even more transcendent transgression.

As with next year's *Lust for Frankenstein*, Franco takes advantage of his new video medium to experiment with some new optical effects. This is, I believe, Franco's first foray into video and he does a great job of adapting to his new medium and making it work for him. The film is every bit as strong visually as any number of Franco's films, but in its own bold new way.

Franco's noteworthy use of trippy music is readily apparent here. By virtue of his penchant for creating visual mesmerism and aural hypnotics—both in typical high gear here—Franco has passed with flying colors the risky segue from film to shooting on video. This is a medium that is quite far from beloved in the eyes of a number of cinema aficionados.

Some of the several intense and captivating tableaus on view in *Tender Flesh* are scored with an unusual blend of slow, soft, ethereally psychedelic music featuring the siren-like "ooohing" voice of a woman, along with weird bits from a strange talking noise in the background. The texture is hypnotic.

The score provides a fitting accompaniment to the electric but low-key erotica that greets the eye frequently in *Tender Flesh*, a film that

saw Franco moving forward, adapting to the new video medium technology and working synergistically with these changes to find amazing new avenues for expressing his exceptional creative film voice, an utterly unique cinematic personality.
And Franco mingles, in a soft way, violence and sensuality.
And again, there is no shock forthcoming.
A single striking example that sticks heavy in the brain, due to its contrast with the excesses of other scenes, is that of a woman with some S&M-induced scars being kindly attended to by another nude woman. Her caretaker in the buff tends to the injured woman's wounds and provides erotically-fueled caresses to boot.
Franco is really in his element with this oddity. The shift to video is bound to be jarring for some. Even for me it was a strange experience.
But to my mind the discovery of the bizarre mysteries of where the director will lead us next, of what unknown veils he will tear down—to reveal even greater mysteries of art and spirit, is a major part of what makes Franco's filmmaking compelling.

Jess Franco's *Tender Flesh* is a cinematic slap in the face—and I mean that in such a good way.
Even the most experienced—jaded, if you prefer—consumer of this director's work will find room to be shocked and surprised in this *The Most Dangerous Game* retooling.
In fact this new media of video, whose visual mien is markedly different than the grain of film, brings a curious new patina to a cinematic style we know all too well.
For a director who has shocked and shocked again, the wonderful opportunity offered by the challenging new video medium benefits both the director and the viewer. Jess Franco is blessed to be able to re-experience his vivid artistic self-expression all over again in fresh, bold fashion and we viewers receive the thrill of experiencing a sharp new jolt from this great art house filmmaker.

FEMALE VAMPIRE (1973)

Now here is a movie that lays bare—right down to the bone—some of Jess Franco's favorite themes:
- ✓ heightened emphasis on the innate sexual nature of the vampire
- ✓ oodles of atmosphere
- ✓ the presentation of graphic and transgressive depictions of human sexuality mingled with heady, potent themes of violence, in a way that both titillates *and* enlightens.

This movie also functions as a striking love affair/homage to Lina Romay, his muse during the second half of his career. She is on display in the nude, or nearly so, for much of the film. Additionally, *Female Vampire* is one of the major Franco films that most closely resembles soft core pornography.

To the uninitiated, that is. Franco's films were frequently chock full of soft core visuals. This one is particularly strong in that regard. But it still isn't porn, however much the deluge of bold soft core imagery is on tap. In fact, there really is a loving touch to the whole affair.

The movie opens with an ethereal score and a foggy wooded scene. A woman's voice sings wordlessly over what unfolds onscreen. White mist fills the space between trees. It is a haunting scene.

From the depths of the fog emerges what is quite plainly a vampiress (Lina Romay). She is clad in big boots, a belt, a cape and little more. Her luscious, full breasts and her soft, pale skin cast their allure beyond where the eyes can see, penetrating the mists with intensity and grabbing us by the balls.

The film takes a slow appraisal of the female vampire once she is near the camera (which she bumps at one point—something that I will explain in a moment). The camera's eye, at close range, moves slowly and lovingly down the height of her body and then back up. This opening is an unabashed and frank appraisal of the delights of the female form and is a promise of things to come.

Now, briefly, one could blame or criticize the *apparent* "blunder" of Franco's camera-bumping vampire; the incident is too obvious to have been missed by the director. I think it is part of Franco's penchant for upsetting film narrative in shocking ways. What supplies more of a jolt to cinematic narrative than not only a fourth-wall break, but a particularly egregious break?

A bumped camera is a flagrant violation of Wall #4, one whose deliberate inclusion is not the result of contrarian writing, but instead a channeled dada instinct to retain—after the fact—what might have been purely accidental.

Even for Franco, this film is a very direct and bold look at sexuality and sensuality—and that is saying something. *Female Vampire*'s resounding artistic success is in great part due to the very matter-of-fact way he steps up and peers so honestly and unashamedly at female sexuality.

I think that among Franco's most well-known (relatively speaking) films, this may be one of those most easily mistaken as pornography by

FEMALE VAMPIRE

Lina Romay (right) stars as the *Female Vampire*.

the uninitiated.

This is a matter probably exacerbated by the existence—in bootleg and gray market circles—of an X-rated version of *Female Vampire*, created by a distributor who added scenes of penetration (which plainly are not part of the original film) to scenes of only a soft core graphic nature.

Rather than spiraling into hyped-up, gonzo art house mania with a number of his super-erotic efforts, Franco maintains a more restrained mode here. And the film's cinematography seems calmer, somehow more still, while continuing to move—Franco has little truck with extended stationary camera shots.

The restraint shown by Franco creates, as I said, a very matter-of-fact feeling in the film's approach.

The film threatens, at least for less understanding cinema-goers, to suggest to the mind an oblique surface resemblance between the deceitfully straightforward (we use the term loosely) approach on view here versus the utter matter-of-factness of sheer pornography, whose camera is used mostly to frame the sex.

Franco loves contrast—this we know—and very early in *Female Vampire* we are presented with our first example.

Once we have seen the ethereal opening credits sequence that introduces us to the vampiress, the film promptly takes us to Countess Irina (for that is her name) making her first kill.

Where Stoker buried the sexual component of vampires mostly in the novel's subtext, Jess Franco, in this film, presents one of his most upfront expositions on the sexual nature of a vampire attack.

Most vampires go for the throat. Irina, however, goes for the cock. She is a vampire with a helluva libido and a helluva fellatio fetish. Her vampiric attacks are overtly sexual seductions.

As if to place a particularly subversive tenor of un-death in the un-life of a vampire, one of Irina's doomed bedmates, after presumably dying pretty damn happy, continues to be fucked by the Countess, whose sexual rapaciousness seems nigh unbounded.

This is quite a beautifully deranged sequence, watching the vampiress ride the drained—and, yes, pun intended—male victim after his life has been bled from him. I would argue that Franco may have understood the true nature of the vampire as well as or better than anybody in the world of film.

One peculiar but fascinating sequence is that of Irina, who is the last of the Karlstein family, being interviewed by a reporter.

It is an odd stacking of contrasts—from the fantastical dark horror of erotica to the reporter's interview, which although both glamorous and exciting in terms of media and celebrity, is also terribly mundane when contrasted with what we've already seen.

This interview with a vampire (regardless of whether or not the reporter knows Irina's nature) is just the sort of artful and banal absurdism Franco inserts into his pictures time and again to stand juxtaposed against the more fantastical elements of a film.

And of course, *Female Vampire* becomes another of Franco's successes in presenting beauty with deviant thrills—a *ménage à trois* between the viewer and the ever inseparable Eros and Thanatos.

Lest you fear Franco has forgotten his fondness for Sapphic activity, you will be more than pleased to note that Irina gets a kick out of stalking chicks, too. And, yes, Irina also digs cunnilingus.

I should also mention the fact that *Female Vampire* is one of Franco's many exercises in creating lavish style from minimalist approaches. The settings are lovely but low-key, the music not frenzied or overly complex, and what "special effects" there are involve little more than basic creative editing.

In so doing, Franco has created a movie touched with a certain unassuming lushness and it is one of his more well known and noteworthy films.

Really, it is hard to go wrong with anything of a vampiric nature that issues from the mind of Franco and becomes emblazoned in celluloid or imposed on a block of pixels—the man did go video in the last phase of his career.

Profane versus mundane, death versus sex, minimalism versus ostentation, beauty versus beastliness ... Franco is in fine form with this piece of cinema.

It is worth pointing out that the seduction/sex scenes are, or at least feel, quite prolonged. Maybe these scenes are not any longer than in plenty of other Franco flicks, but they have a much more subdued tone (by Franco standards)—sometimes there is no score over the sex and therefore the long nature of the erotic encounters in his films is more highlighted.

This subdued tone adds to that matter-of-factness that taunts us by shamelessly flaunting a superficial similarity to porn while being anything but.

Honestly, if I had a friend that I wished to turn on to the ecstasies of Jess Franco and was concerned that my friend would readily jump to the porno assumption if I didn't ease him into Franco's shocking canon, then I am fairly certain that I would start by showing him *Female Vampire*.

I think it is reasonably fair to say that acceptance requires a little more maturity in the heart that digs Franco—by which I mean I think it is best to start elsewhere and work up to the paradoxical headiness of his tonally more low-key efforts.

One of the most startling things to behold in this film—and one of its most memorable scenes—is that in which a lone Irina makes long, slow, deliberate love to her bed.

Not that she jams a bedpost up her vagina or anything as ghastly as that, but the countess sure as hell shows you how phallic a symbol the bedpost is.

And by employing musical cues from previous encounters of the sexual variety, Franco lends this bizarre sequence as much tenderness and erotic credibility as any of the person-on-person encounters preceding this.

Of course, what the filmmaker is doing here is using hyperbole to wordlessly express the glory of autoeroticism.

The thrills of masturbation and self-pleasuring frequently involve foreign objects—a dildo, for example, or other grown-up toys.

A bed is also a foreign object, although this seems a bit ridiculous at first.

But this is an example of Franco's hyperbolic expression of the intense joys of self-pleasure and he is adjuring us to apologize to absolutely no one for the strangeness of our sexual peccadilloes.

The director also uses the classic pillow between the legs, only this pillow is big, long and cylindrical, in other words, a huge phallic symbol.

Meanwhile, the police try to figure out who the hell is going around oral-sexing folks to death!

Franco, unsurprisingly, brings a striking sequence of erotic S&M into the film's narrative, and Irina is one of the people being whipped.

This scene is quite sexually charged, of course, as a woman flogs the vampiress, who endures the lashing impassively.

This is something of a unique S&M scene, even for Jess Franco, although he has shot far more intense scenes of sadomasochism.

Female Vampire is not only a romantic-feeling headlong dive into the thrilling and frightful union of sex and death, but also a luxurious bath in the rushing waters that shape the morbid into beauty—which actually means uncovering the beauty that already exists in what we see as morbid.

The story draws to a close with a scene right out of the legend of Countess Bathory, as we see Irina luxuriating with electric sensuality in a bath of blood.

And then the deadly, dangerous and delectable female vampire disappears back into the fog from whence she first appeared.

THE DEMONS (1973)

Never has Jess Franco showed cinematic fear when portraying sadism or even cruelty, the two not always being the same. *The Demons* is far from being an exception to this statement.

The film features Howard Vernon as an aristocrat balls deep in this sordid affair; as we have seen, Vernon worked with Franco many times. *The Demons* also features the lovely Britt Nichols and Anne Libert, both of whom have worked with the director elsewhere, including another 1973 film, *Cristina, Princess of Eroticism*, aka *A Virgin Among the Living Dead*.

It is entirely unsurprising that Franco took a turn at nunsploitation cinema. This is a cruel genre that he wholly embraced and made his own. Having already produced pioneering works in the women-in-prison genre, it comes as no surprise that he is equally adept at exploring cruelty and sadism in a dark erotic piece such as *The Demons*.

The opening sequence depicts the brutality of the Inquisition as holy witchfinders look for spots on a woman's tongue, poke her with a needle (because if she reacts, hey, she's a witch!) and pour hot, scalding water on her breasts.

Which begs a few questions:
- ✓ Why would a non-witch's boobs be safe from scalding water?
- ✓ Were the sanctified tests of the Inquisitors supposed to be harmless if applied to non-witches?
- ✓ Didn't they start to wonder when their tests had a 100% conviction rate?
- ✓ Or did they think they were as good at rooting out witches as swine are at snuffling out truffles?

The Inquisition itself seemed mostly useful as an excuse for being cruel. If you are an inquisitor, by definition, you cannot not be guilty of sin: all acts are done in the name of God and the Holy Mother Church. I honestly suspect that on a subconscious, collective scale, this was the church working furiously to root out the sacred feminine, which had been largely repressed—except in the blade-of-grass-through-concrete kind of way, like the cult of Mary and her co-mediatrix status with Jesus, aka God, and the personification of wisdom as Sophia.

But while the Inquisition was doubtless nothing more than the execution of cruelty and misogyny under the blasphemous guise of holy acts committed for a demanding God, Franco's movie *about* the Inquisition is much more than an excuse to wallow in cruelty.

Needless to say, *The Demons* contains some broad satire of hypocritical organized religion and humanity's infuriating tendency to mistake evil for good, and good for evil—but it also delivers a chilling thrill ride into the shadows and into our personal shadows.

What we witness in this film is the fearless revelation of the dark nature we all harbor to varying degrees. Franco is fascinating us and terrifying us by showing us our own nature. It is a dreadful mirror into which we peer.

Franco's criticism explores not only the religious sector of culture, but also the mores of society that extend into and penetrate the secular realm, as well. In other words, the filmmaker targets all the so-called ethical standards of our world which reveal themselves as rank hypocrisy rather than being true spiritual or moral standards.

On another level, *The Demons* is about repression.

And not only the imposition of social parameters upon the free-thinking individual, but also the repression of the ubermensch who threatens the herd's way of life. Additionally, the film portrays personal repression, which is, of course, at least partially the result of imposed familial and social moral norms.

But while society helps to shape our code of ethics (even if it forges us into iconoclasts rather than embracers of standard social mores), we can also be guilty of trapping ourselves in our own cages of false morality.

Therefore, at some point of our understanding as we grow and learn, we become responsible for continuing to cling to what has been passed down, to customize it to ourselves, or to reject it entirely.

A specific example of defining a moral position, as portrayed in *The Demons*, is the reaction of authority to autoeroticism.

We see convent members who have suddenly taken to indulging in some quite steamy self-knowledge, but masturbatory behavior is immediately placed in the context of being "wrong".

And with religious strictures replacing general socio-cultural moral repression, masturbation is here presented not only as inherently wrong, but as a classic—one dare say archetypal—symbol of shame attached to an act, that from a different perspective, is wholesome, natural and 100% God-approved.

And masturbation here is representative of all acts that are right and proper of themselves, but which society has fearfully labeled as shameful behavior.

Don't you ever wonder if the strong undercurrents of S&M culture in our society may be blades of grass breaking through the concrete of American culture's dishonest puritanical heritage?

We can lie about ourselves and wear what Anton LaVey referred to as the "good guy badge", pretending to be "good"—whatever that may mean—rather than actually just doing good—forgetting entirely about excessively Zoroastrian dichotomies and simply accepting ourselves while pursuing spiritual and psychological growth, rather than focusing on moral spectrums.

Now, on an entirely different note, how do you feel about using a torture implement that sort of resembles a pair of garden shears to cut a woman's breast while someone demands that she admit to liking it?

There is also a mace-like sort of object that the torturer rolls down the naked nun's torso, leaving marks where the spikes have gouged her.

No reason Franco shouldn't be as graphic in his depictions of Thanatos as he is his presentations of Eros.

Most of the time, I feel like Franco devotes more cinematic explicitness to his erotic scenes than he does his horror scenes. The horror component of his work forms more of an umbrella presence, or else is expressed in relatively less graphic ways.

(There are, quite naturally, exceptions.)

For that matter, what is seen in this film, strictly on the level of visual violence, is far less graphic than we see in *Bloody Moon*, Franco's tip of the hat to the American slasher film. *Bloody Moon* may actually be one of his most violently graphic films.

But what makes the violence in *The Demons* so disturbing lies in its cruel nature and the particularly harsh juxtaposition of sex and death as it is played out.

This film is an example of a particularly visceral and invasive film within Jess Franco's canon. When a poor nun is rudely and ruthlessly probed to verify the intactness of her maidenhead, the viewer feels nearly as mortified and violated as the nun.

Maybe those overzealous priests and nuns should not have gotten such a kick out of burning that witch.

We learn that this outburst of supposedly blasphemous behavior is due to a curse the witch spat out as the flames were consuming her body. Her tormentors presumably had their erotic urges well under check before all this.

As appalled as the Inquisitors must have been by this outbreak of cursed and libidinous nuns, I'm sure they were delighted in equal measures by all the torturous fun in store for them as they "tested" each of the suspect horny habit-wearing women.

This isn't exactly the same type of sadism presented in some of Franco's S&M paeans to pain. In these other works we find that the subtextual thrust is often about the birth-pangs of self-discovery and, further, the thrilling terror of discovering one's heretofore hidden unorthodox desires.

In *The Demons*, it is not the use of S&M as self-discovery that we observe, but pure sadism for its own sake—inflicted upon unwilling women—and in truth, nothing but misogynistic sadism.

I realize I would be laughed out of many film discussions by saying this, but I will say it: *The Demons*, if you look deep and have eyes that you may see, you will realize that this film is, on one level, a *feminist film*.

This is the same kind of truth that can be used to describe Meir Zarchi's *Day of the Woman* (aka *I Spit on Your Grave*). The deluded have decried the film as a worthless piece of female-hating misogyny. But the film is actually a work of feminist cinema: dig its original title, a title less sensational and more appropriate than the one the distributor slapped on it. And yes, men can create feminist works.

By the way, I am sure the Inquisitor's forceful screwing of a naughty nun was strictly a punishment meted down by God and executed by his representative on the earth. I mean, it's a dirty job and somebody has to do it. How can a man of God refuse to do what the Lord has called upon him to do?

Right?

The Demons is not a mean-spirited movie—it is a movie *about* meanness. On a more universal level, Franco has created a treatment on fear in general—nothing to fear but fear itself—and how the things that scare us most are sometimes just we needlessly scaring ourselves.

So many of our fears are based on the undeserved power we attribute to a thing, rather than the actual power of the thing itself. We are, frequently, our own worst enemies.

And as ugly a topic as is on display here and however compelling the subject matter might be (and if we are honest with ourselves), we see that Franco remains undaunted in addressing a corrosive subject with a real sense of beauty, and he does it with his amazing minimalist panache.

The Demons also features a blind oracle figure—as does *Christina, Princess of Eroticism*—only in this movie she is a wife of Satan.

It is a sharp twist of Franco's satirical knife that the character who stands as an enemy of the Church is a wife of Satan! Her actions are ironically evil as she sets up church minions as the true villains of the piece.

The oracle—a voice of wisdom—is of the family of the Devil. This represents a massive middle-finger aimed at the Church, a ruthless upending of conventional Christian morality.

The Demons comes from several directions in its assault on moral hypocrisy: the framing of something innocent as something evil and, what is worse, using the perversion of innocence as a mechanism for control, rather than as a mechanism for ethical guidance or mentoring.

Franco's films are forever unflinching.

The tortures inflicted upon the characters in this film are a direct indictment of the cruelties, various and sundry, mankind will enjoy, even while denying the cruelty of these acts.

The film is also an unreserved portrayal of our own selves as seen through a fictional hyperbole rooted in the historical Inquisition, whose extremes have become synonymous with cruelty, not to mention a reminder of the potentially darker side of religion, another thing usually innocent in and of itself, but …

And just as the Inquisition is an actual in-history example of the truly hyperbolic, but all too real expressions of depraved human cruelty, Franco's *The Demons* is a cinematic piece of "excess", a conscious exercise in the hyperbole of fiction based upon the viciousness recorded in our history books.

Both the actual Inquisition and Franco's fictional portrayal blatantly show us the harsh realities of human cruelty. The historical Inquisition was not attempting to define cruelty for more enlightened successors (all it was trying to demonstrate was the patriarchal power of the Church), but nevertheless it did just that.

Franco makes the same demonstration, but deliberately and through art.

Moving on, I would like to mention that Jess Franco was an equal opportunity torturer (onscreen only, of course); it is not only women who are plied with pain. With a man torturing a man, could we see this as the male repression of sexuality he sees as unfit or shameful?

And since Franco likes to throw the viewer for a loop, toward the end of *The Demons*, the film gets all swashbuckling on us. Suddenly it feels like the Three Musketeers have invaded the erotic art house. Kudos to Franco, as I find this sequence as enjoyable as the rest of the film.

Also, there is a random meowing cat. I have no words at all for how awesome that is.

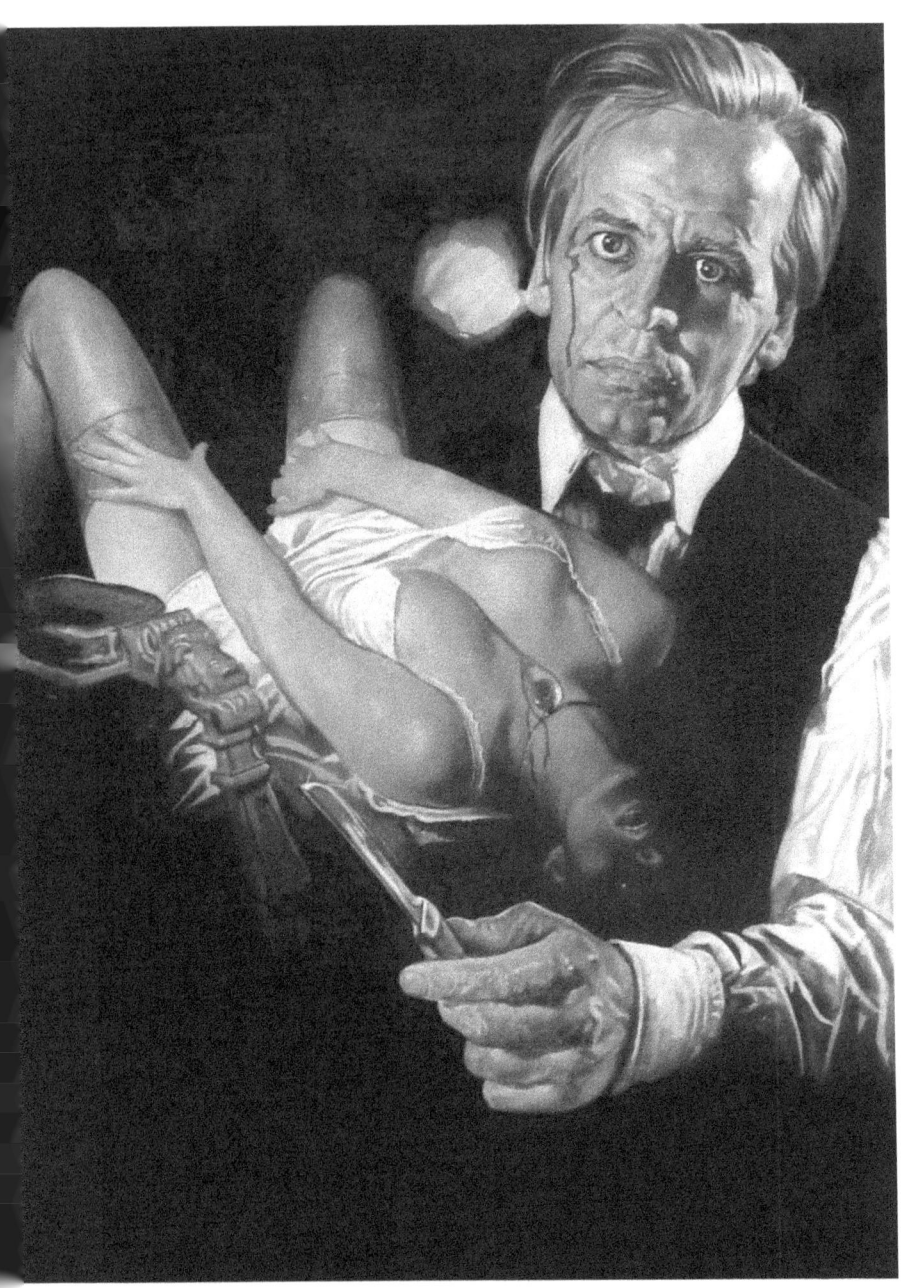

Klaus Kinski stars in *Jack the Ripper*.

JACK THE RIPPER (1976)

Oh boy, how many combinations are cooler than Jess Franco and Klaus Kinski? Not many, I'd wager.

Kinski worked with Franco elsewhere: it was a brilliant choice for Franco to cast the crazy German actor (Werner Herzog's infamous frenemy) as the lunatic Renfield in the director's *Count Dracula*. I also fancy the idea of Kinski playing the Dracula figure in Herzog's luminous *Nosferatu*.

(Historical Note: the vampire is not referred to as "Dracula" in Herzog's film since it was a remake of F.W. Murnau's silent picture *Nosferatu*, which was an unlicensed adaptation of Stoker's novel. The original movie changed some names and plot points, but it was still bloody obvious that it was based on the Stoker book. Because the filmmakers had not paid for the film rights, Stoker's widow tried to have all copies of Murnau's film destroyed. She failed, thankfully.)

And, of course, to see Franco at work on such an iconic historical figure as Jack the Ripper is exciting. Here again, the director turns the material on its ear and presents a unique take on the famous, and as yet unidentified killer.

Jack the Ripper is a far from historically accurate depiction of the serial murderer's real-life blood-shedding—nor is it meant to be.

This film is more concerned with the legend than it is about the man lurking behind the legend. Besides, how many movies make it through the Franco filter without becoming transformed?

That *Count Dracula* is (probably) the most faithful film version of Stoker's book is actually anomalous. The great bulk of Franco's literary borrowings are re-imagined and forged into a vision unique to Franco.

Stanley Kubrick did much the same thing, at least at times. He, too, was known to take the germ of a source story and forge a new cinematic entity. Witness *The Shining*.

Jack the Ripper is closer to being a slasher film than anything else, if we feel like categorizing. As discussed in the chapter on *Bloody Moon*, slashers are not foreign to Franco, but they are not common in his canon, either.

An interesting tweak in the Ripper legend is that of Jack having a somewhat daft housekeeper, who is always delighted when he brings home a hooker's corpse for her to admire, and naturally, to discard for him. Her first onscreen body-dumping excursion comes early in the film when we see her row out on a body of water to dump a big burlap sack full o' body into the water.

But she hesitates. She peeks into the bag with a childlike awe, as though she were an excited tot allowed to rummage through Santa's sack. She pulls out an eyeball. She wants it so bad. As a keepsake.

An interesting non-tweak is that of Franco's depiction of the Ripper as a doctor. This is actually one of the favored hypotheses for the identity of the real Jack—that he was a doctor, thus accounting for the apparent precision evident in his slicing-up of unfortunate ladies of the night.

Making Jack a doctor in this iteration also lets Franco show us a little bit of medical gore, such as the Ripper's rather painful opening of a man's "rotten canker." This a simple FX trick, but it proves effective and gross enough even without any excess ooze.

But you can't really feel bad for the character seeking treatment since he quite plainly intends to rob Jack, evident from the his terribly unsubtle "innocent" questions about the doctor's wealth—of which there is actually little. His patients are poor and just minutes before we have heard him say that he is behind in his rent.

Part of *Jack the Ripper* is constructed as a police procedural. A major early scene shows an uptight old lady getting snippy during questioning; she was witness to some part of the Ripper's latest crime.

But a more interesting witness is a blind man who encountered both a prostitute and the Ripper on the night Jack killed her (this event is shown during the opening credits). The blind man's keen senses and just-as-keen reasoning allow him to put together some significant clues that may help to identify the Ripper—if the man can be found.

Jack the Ripper gives enough screen time to the police procedural aspect of the story to lend it as much significance as that of Jack and the horrible killings themselves. The movie isn't purely interested in only a doctor who is cursed with a bent brain and is running amok with sharp objects in London.

The movie also has its own interesting take on Jack the Ripper's nuttiness. We see that he is prone to hallucinatory visions that reveal to him a beautiful women whispering all sorts of crazy shit in his direction.

(And, lordy, lookee there, a nightclub cabaret scene. You old scoundrel, Franco!)

As per most slasher films, *Jack the Ripper* is punctuated with objects like eyeballs and hands and severed stumps and such, but they do not comprise a dominant aspect of the film. These objects are really just punctuations, something bright and dreadful to insert during the shadowy progressions of this movie's tale. In that sense this film is a bit non-slashery.

   Jack the Ripper is one of Franco's simpler films, but that is no condemnation. I am the last person to balk at simplicity in storytelling. While being less of a Jess Franco mood piece, this film offers a top notch context for the union of sex and death, and the director who loves such themes.

   The Ripper is tempted toward an act of violence outside his norm during the final portion of the film. This is when that pesky, unscrupulous bum with the "rotten canker" tries to blackmail Jack. This creature has managed to suss out the fact that Jack is not just Jack, but Jack the Ripper and so attempts to blackmail him.

   But Jack deviates from his method of killing female victims, out of necessity, to kill his male victim. One of the most shocking scenes in the film is the discovery of the would-be shakedown artist hanging from the rafters, his face gnarled into a painful rictus.

   Ironically, the death of the blackmailer is the least gory death in the picture, but emerges as the most impactful, perhaps by contrast with the quick but violent shots of the prostitutes' gruesome deaths.

   And even this historical police procedural/slasher film receives a caring and wonderful cinematographic treatment even if it is not a spectacle film. Despite its sporadically grisly nature and deliberately dim-lit settings, *Jack the Ripper* is in fact a pretty film.

THE BLOOD OF FU MANCHU (1968)

Yet again, we have even more evidence—as if it was really needed at this point—that Franco was nothing if not versatile. In this film he takes a surprising venture into adapting a famous literary character from Sax Rohmer's vintage espionage/crime fiction about the yellow-peril-era super villain Fu Manchu.

Franco is full of surprises and to find him tackling a rather old school story from an old school literary source (not to mention its subsequent movie legacy) certainly ranks as rather a surprise—except if you factor in the axiom that Franco's canon is full of surprises.

This is one of Franco's many collaborations with Christopher Lee, who (surprisingly!) plays the Asian villain Fu Manchu. Lee owns the film, even though he is surrounded by colorful sets, action and a bevy of beauties.

The Blood of Fu Manchu begins by looking like something the Shaw Brothers might have cooked up for a *wushu* movie. But there is no kung fu here. Instead there is Christopher Lee.

Lee plays the role of Rohmer's classic pulp character Fu Manchu like a James Bond super villain who got his own series. And, yes, I know that having a Brit play Fu Manchu is the kind of thing some people like to get bent out of shape about, but what is important is not skin-color or ethnicity (gasp!) but rather the ability of the actor to play the role. Lee was a powerful actor with a powerful presence and he is his usual brilliant self in this role.

Fu Manchu waxes diabolical as he orders a woman confronted with poisonous snakes drawn from an eerie coffin. He is recruiting people—whether they like it or not—for the advancement of whatever super crazy world domination scheme he has stashed up the sleeves of his oriental robe.

Fu Manchu definitely gives off a kind of evil cult leader vibe.

A film like *The Blood of Fu Manchu* is a golden opportunity for some gorgeous filmmaking and Jess Franco doesn't disappoint. The movie is richly visual, even if it does not have a Spielberg budget. As we have seen, this filmmaker has a long history of crafting beautiful films with relatively limited resources.

If you didn't know better, it may seem surprising that Franco has made an adventure movie. There is even a sequel to *The Blood of Fu Manchu —The Castle of Fu Manchu*—and these are not Franco's only forays into the adventure movie genre. Some of his horror films have adventure movie action components, for example the military flashbacks in *Oasis of the Zombies* and the fisticuffs and gunfights seen in *Devil Hunter*. Both movies are discussed elsewhere in this book.

So Fu Manchu employs ten deadly ... hotties? Yes, indeed. They are tasked with bringing gifts (gifts that go kill, maybe?) to various targets in the villain's sights. As it happens, this gift is something that many a man would welcome—a kiss from a voluptuous woman—except that, alas, these ladies' kisses are of the deadly kind.

The act of gift giving also proves deadly for the voluptuous killers. As we see, once a poison-lipped female assassin does her duty, she is offed. The first kiss-killer in the film is run down by a car with a masked person behind the wheel as soon as she leaves her victim's house. No loose ends, I suppose.

I don't know if Fu Manchu did this in any of the books, but it is a capital idea and one right down Franco's alley. One can also describe this movie as, in part, a piece of film noir. That is a genre that is pretty uncommon in the director's canon, but Franco-does-noir is a welcome

Christopher Lee and a bevy of deadly beauties in *The Blood of Fu Manchu.*

experience.

This movie also reminds me a bit of the old chapter plays. There is something about the scenes in Fu Manchu's lair that call to mind the film serials of the 30s and 40s. It is always refreshing and invigorating to see Franco step just a little outside his already eclectic "norm."

At times, in *The Blood of Fu Manchu*, there is also a notable lightheartedness and quirky sense of humor evident. But the film is at its best during the gothic scenes in Fu Manchu's lair. The use of color and the clever framing of the spartan sets make this film yet another delicious example of gothic cinema from a director skilled in the delivery of such yummy film treats.

While the whole time treating themes and cinematic/narrative ideas that pop up repeatedly in the director's movies, this is a distinctive film among its Franco-helmed peers. Franco is a challenge for several reasons:

- ✓ the opacity of many of his great surrealist efforts
- ✓ his application of intense, graphic erotica in non-pornographic contexts (although I have read that he shot a little porn)
- ✓ his discomfiting fusion of Eros and Thanatos in often highly transgressive ways
- ✓ in this film, the wide reach of his directorial eye and the resultant diversity that informs his body of work.

Beauties in peril, colorful characters and costumes, gothic tones, loads of mood ... and Christopher Lee in one of his more striking roles.

There is a bit of sadism and torture here, too. Not that any Franco fanatic would be shocked. A man is tested with a device that threatens to put spikes through him. A woman, her breasts stripped bare, endures the pressing of a poisonous snake against her bosom (yes, the snake bites). Franco can always stretch himself—and always his artistic presence is omnipresent in his movies, regardless of the direction his love of versatility reaches.

WOMEN BEHIND BARS (1975)

Franco did several women in prison movies, among them this one. I am sure the title was a dead giveaway. The muse for the second part of his career—Lina Romay—takes center stage here. But while we are often led to feel much sympathy for the confined-and-tortured female victims in this type of picture, Lina Romay performs in this film as a woman with a deadly criminal secret. She is hardly innocent and one might see her subsequent afflictions as fair karma (although we hardly like her tormentors).

At the beginning of the movie we see a heist gone wrong when the heist-man is killed by his wife (Romay), who pockets the loot. She is soon off to a prison in the tropics, however, where you know things will get nasty quick. A stash like a mondo valuable passel of jewels is a hard thing to keep secret, and the trials she faces in the land of sadism-behind-bars will threaten to undo all her plans.

In simplest terms, this is a brutal story of greed and murder punished.

Even while Romay is suffering her torments inside the jail, the proverbial walls are closing in from the outside on the corrupt prison authorities. An investigator sent by the insurers of the swiped gems is convinced of a connection between the murder and the heist. He doggedly sets out to find the truth.

Meanwhile, there is nowhere for Romay's wicked wife character to flee. Even if she escapes the cruelties of her captors, she will be pursued by the determined insurance man once she is on the outside.

Here again (and again), Franco ably employs simplicity to achieve compelling cinematography. For example, two people and a table shot with the right composition render an attention-getting image. Franco also inserts some psychological cat-and-mouse head games amidst the looming doom. The warden takes a very special interest in the jewel-stashing husband-killer. But what he tries to play off as curiosity or professional interest is a falsehood easily seen through.

Romay knows he wants to know the location of the gemstones. And being completely under his control, where can she hide from whatever cruelty he wishes to unleash on her? Schemes of sneaky plotting combined with overt pain are launched to make an attempt at snagging the info required to locate the treasure.

The warden is not above wooing another female prisoner with the promise of improved prison conditions in order to (a) gratify his own sexual pleasure, and (b) send his seduced inmate lover to make friends with the hubby-killer and dig up some facts.

The inter-personal dynamics become even more complicated and compelling when the insurance man shows up at the prison to speak with the woman with a secret. With all these conflicting motives at work in such a volatile scenario, the match is about to be applied to the dynamite fuse. Franco works up some gut-grabbing suspense as the insurance guy enters the jail with considerable trepidation. He's got a bad feeling. As do we, the viewers. This is a potent powder keg and it could explode in any direction.

Women Behind Bars is not as overwrought as a lot of women in prison films and it is a calmer film than much of Franco's other work. What helps is a layer of melodrama the director successfully infuses into a film whose genre is not exactly known for effective dramatic efforts.

Jess Franco has so many tricks up his sleeves.

The relative chill factor of *Women Behind Bars* is broken with a helluva mean whipping sequence. It is disturbing that the naked back (and backside) of a woman could still provoke an erotic response in the midst of a sadistic flogging—a form of punishment I find particularly gut-twisting. But that speaks to Franco's ability to show us our dark halves and, not only that, to make us kind of like it, even if we feel just a little tingle. In multi-faceted and uncanny ways, the filmmaker is able to lay bare our most tenebrous inner selves.

Following the flogging, a sharply contrasting tenderness emerges as two of the female inmates find sensual solace in each other. A very Francoan study in contrast.

A subtle and small touch that somehow forcefully drives home the heart of this movie: as a bitchy, butchy female guard is getting all aggro on an inmate for some insipid, miniscule infraction, a call to stand for prayer is issued! This scene certainly recalls Franco in Inquisition mode in *The Demons*. Cruelty is just fucking dandy provided a blessing is said over the damn thing.

Oh, and don't dare get caught passing a note during mealtime. It's straight off to the punishment cell for you and you sure as hell won't like that one damn bit.

I dare say this is a superior entry in the WIP genre, a genre that Franco helped to forge. This movie has the staple themes of the women in prison film, but the heist plot used as a pivot on which the WIP material works, as well as the surprisingly "serious" tone with which the story is told, really makes this a particularly interesting example of this genre.

Leave it to Mr. Jess Franco, right?

The first overt torture of the black widow Romay is very, very jarring.

A guard is told to apply the pain, and he begins to fiddle with what looks like a soundboard. This device, it turns out, controls electrodes attached to her inner thighs, very high up, very near the genitalia. It is quite a disturbing scene.

For all its simplicity, this is one of the most horribly horrifying things I have ever seen in one of Jess Franco's movies. And still, Franco finds time to tease the erotic out from nothing more than the sleeping forms of women behind bars. His shadow/light dichotomy is unrivaled.

And a quote: "I find you as beautiful when you're laughing as when you're suffering."

It is as though Franco has discovered a way to insert and encapsulate the core philosophy behind all his Marquis de Sade inspired works (and other thematically related titles) within the confines of a single sentence in *Women Behind Bars*. The man is a marvel—I might have said it before somewhere but it truly bears repeating. He astounds me with how he can find so many fresh and exotic ways of exploring his themes multiple times without seeming repetitive.

In its unassuming way, *Women Behind Bars* stands tall, shoulder to shoulder with some of Franco's finest works.

Fittingly enough, the movie concludes on a note that quietly but powerfully challenges conventional moral sensibilities and shatters ideas of the strict black-and-white rigidity of such morality. For all his exploration of dualities upon dualities, Franco ultimately uses this cinematic questing to push beyond this duality and into a mystical union of ideas.

DEVIL HUNTER (1980)

Devil Hunter has a special place in my heart. This film represents the first Jess Franco movie I ever saw a piece of, and there is a really interesting story on how that happened.

In the 80s, during the height of the video era—which I sorely miss—my Dad was anxious to see *Manhunter*, the latest Michael Mann film and the first film adaptation of Thomas Harris' *Red Dragon*, so he called a local video store and reserved a copy to rent. At the time, however, Franco's *Devil Hunter* was available in America on VHS under the title *Man Hunter*. By the time we got to the scene where a kidnapper takes a big curvy blade to a stolen starlet's tit, my Dad already knew damn well this was the wrong movie and that he sure as shit didn't want to watch any more of the awful thing.

Boy, was he pissed.

But for me it was the planting of a seed. A seed which took a long time to germinate, but here I am writing a book on Franco. It was a long time before I saw the full, uncut movie. Since then I've watched it a number of times. It is one of those terrific Jess Franco movies far too easily dismissed as bad camp by those who fail to catch the director's gonzo vibe. And this is definitely jungle horror/action of mondo gonzo status.

There is a monster in the jungle and it has big, bulging, bloodshot eyes. He registers as pretty primitive and vicious, running around buck-ass nekkid and he really digs it when the fearful villagers tie up one of their women as a sacrifice to him. He gets hungry.

This is one of the most out-there examples of the cannibal film genre. *Devil Hunter* even eschews the established formula for jungle cannibal fare, as established by Umberto Lenzi (*The Man From Deep River*, *Cannibal Ferox*) and Ruggero Deodato (*Cannibal Holocaust*). Not that there is any good reason whatsoever that the likes of Franco should not deviate from the template.

Devil Hunter is not just horror-in-the-jungle. It is also action in the jungle, and boasts some intrigue, as well. When the aforementioned starlet is kidnapped, her captors hide out on the island where the guy with the bloodshot-ping-pong-ball eyes lives. In their defense, they don't know that there is a big, naked guy running around looking—with his big-ass, bugged-out eyeballs—for people to chow on.

Complications ensue when a man is hired to ransom the kidnapped actress and makes his way to the island to find not only the enemies he expected—the kidnappers—but also this kooky cannibal humanoid. There is machine gun action, cruel eroticism and bizarre cannibalism and monster-movie shenanigans afoot. This is Jess Franco in full-gear.

Despite the abundant themes *Devil Hunter* has in common with many other genre films, it is actually a pretty unique horror film. It is one-of-a-kind even in Franco's catalog of crazy cinematic insanity. And it is one of my favorite films by this delightfully deviant filmmaker. This film almost deserves a category of its own but I wouldn't know what the hell to call it.

Franco creates an interesting tunnel-vision effect for the POV shots depicting the monster's vision. The center of the frame is clear, but all the surrounding area is blurred. I suspect petroleum jelly on the lens, an old trick for soft picture effects and such.

The story becomes a three-way struggle between the kidnappers, the would-be rescuer and the monster, whose passion for eating human flesh is portrayed simply, but strikingly, early in the picture. One of the deviations from most cannibal-jungle flicks is the fact that here, the natives really aren't much of a risk. They are damn near the least dangerous thing in the movie.

Franco created a fine piece of bizarre originality when he shot this

Ursula Buchfellner being menaced in *The Devil Hunter*.

movie. Credit also goes to Franco for making the gunfire-riddled showdown between the captors and the rescuer during a failed money-for-prisoner exchange every bit as exciting as the tense showdown between the hero and the monster atop a steep precipice.

And, you know what? For once, not all the white people lost in the cannibal jungle are stupid white people. We have yet another refreshing Jess Franco twist for a genre whose practically universal moral-of-the-story is that stupid and arrogant white folks shouldn't go barging into the jungle to try to impose their cultural values on a more "primitive" civilization. What happens in *Devil Hunter* comprises an entirely different dynamic altogether.

After a while I think both parties of white folks—kidnappers and rescuers—finally realize that they have a mutual enemy of more concern than other white people. Their situation becomes an ordeal for survival. Get off the island without (a) being eaten or (b) getting shot. And the ransom money is still in play just to keep things a little more anxious.

The movie works just as well as adventure cinema as it does as cannibal cinema, but the combination, merged as only Jess Franco could have done it, is a heady brew.

There is a scene in which one of the kidnappers—who finds out he isn't the badass he thought he was—discovers the bloody bodies of his fellow kidnappers. There are no complicated FX in play, just possum-playing actors and some blood. But the scene works great, and we see a brief flash of the kind of thing we would see in American slashers which were on their way to rocketing popularity at the same time this film was made.

Another slasheresque scene involves a pair of love makers getting interrupted by the killer—in this case the bug-eyed monster. Sex morphs into death. A graphic guts-fondling shot caps the scene.

This is a great movie. Few films are this original and—it is worth reiterating—this is a unique work even by Franco's standards. If you know filmmaker Jess Franco, then you also know that is a ballsy statement to make.

The director includes some scenes of pure mesmerism, as well he should. These scenes include nude tribal dances by the natives, whose totem poll makes it clear that the monster is something of a dark god to them. They both fear and worship it.

Sounds a bit like the all too common misconception people have regarding the Christian deity … don't you think?

THE AWFUL DR. ORLOFF (1962)

A classic, repeated theme in some of older horror's better films is that of the mad scientist whose research is focused irrationally on the restoration of a loved one's scarred skin, no matter how many other women he has to trap and kill to support his mad scientist plastic surgery endeavors.

The Awful Dr. Orloff, one of Franco's early linear works, is the director's version of the oft-told tale (see the French film *Eyes Without a Face* for a classic example). This film isn't a direct remake of any previous versions, *per se*, but it does share the core concept.

So here we have the intersection of a classic horror theme by a director who would become known for his uber-progressive filmmaking.

Dr. Orloff sends his silent henchman Morpho Lodner out to kidnap gorgeous women so he can use them as guinea pigs in his experiments. Despite being a non-speaking role, Morpho is a standout character with his crazily bugged-out eyes and scarred visage.

Dr. Orloff is played by none other than Howard Vernon, who would go on to collaborate with Franco throughout the director's career. Creepy Morpho is portrayed by Ricardo Valle.

This is a prophetic movie, presciently using the fear of science that had helped define sci-fi and horror in the 50s to touch on today's popular controversy regarding cosmetic surgery. The film commences with a skittering, percussive avant-jazz score, floating camera, weird drunken utterances from the woman onscreen (all of which can be seen as prophetic of Franco's later stylish flourishes).

The musical score is damned unsettling and sets your nerves on edge and backs a sudden attack by a blind man—eyes wide open and staring sightlessly—who is in a closet waiting for his inebriated victim. This blind assailant is, of course, Morpho.

This is an awfully strong opening.

The hypnotically beautiful black-and-white photography is a great contributor to the pervasive, foreboding mood of the film. This early in his career, Franco was already mastering the art of creating atmosphere. *The Awful Dr. Orloff* has got to be one of the filmmaker's most beautiful movies, and you already see his transformative talent for taking that which is spartan and transforming it into lush beauty.

A bright young detective is handed a very serious major case by his superior. There are now, he is informed, five vanished women in only twenty days' time. The young police officer is stunned but ready to tackle such an important, challenging and intriguing case. One sees police procedural subplots pop up frequently in Franco's films.

One also sees any number of nightclub scenes in his works too, including one in this movie. Franco is already gearing up for the things he does best. I think it says quite a bit about a filmmaker that one of the man's very earliest works can be ranked among his very best by many Franco fans. (Interestingly, Franco himself did not consider this one of his finer works.)

Another classic Franco motif already in full force in *The Awful Dr. Orloff* is his expert knack for creating doom-laden, atmosphere-drenched gothic cinema. This movie shows him already excelling at this, as well. It is as if he came into the world loaded with a lifetime of singular movie talent.

Here, too, is Franco's stunning cinematography. Some of his finest

Morpho (Ricardo Valle) in *The Awful Dr. Orlof*.

visuals may be found in *Orloff*. Additionally his use of music to maintain mood and suspense, to keep the nerves on edge when necessary, is manifested here and is fully formed. Jess Franco is nothing short of a master of his craft.

Even though this film does not prepare the newcomer to Franco for the psychedelic delights encountered as one digs deeper into the man's canon, it is still absolutely a must-see for anybody sincerely interested in the director's work. For all the natural talent Franco shows when filming his movies in color, his work in black-and-white is just as striking. Shot after shot, *The Awful Dr. Orloff* captivates the eyes and keeps us guessing along with the strange story.

Any discussion of gothic horror is simply left unfinished if Jess Franco has not been introduced into the conversation. *Orloff* is also a reminder of Franco's ability to be equally deft with both surrealistic and linear, more plot-centric narratives. In that regard, this film has its own special place on the shelf right next to the director's *Count Dracula* or *The Diabolical Dr. Z*.

To boot, this movie has a particular focus, in a minor way, on the laughable folly of humans. Human folly is not a primary theme, but by way of example, there is a witty, humorous scene in which the authorities try to coax a useful drawing of the man supposedly seen carting off the ladies, but they end up being frustrated. The scene carries a delightful tongue-in-cheek tone, and this subtlety is the perfect touch to make the sequence go off without a hitch.

Also, a drunk who has some information pertinent to the missing girl case is one of the best characters in the film. He represents one of the strongest characters, in terms of dramatic gravitas. But his dramatic heft also has a light touch. The drunk provides great comic relief—ironically turning the focus of human folly on a police officer and away from himself, even though a drunk would be a stereotypical and classic target for poking fun at humanity's capacity for sheer idiocy.

Here, though, the drunk is a free spirit, and a sincere one. He knows who he is and accepts it without shame. This wino, in his way, anchors the film and its characters. He very nearly serves as the voice of wisdom at the center of all these crazy events. And this extends not so much from anything he says but rather in how he carries himself.

Franco was practically out of the gate at top speed, his talent already sharp-edged. *Orloff* is the work of a genius auteur.

The Awful Dr. Orloff is nothing short of a cinema masterpiece.

VENUS IN FURS (1969)

Inspired by the classic 1870 novel about masochism by Leopold von Sacher-Masoch (from whose name we derive the word "masochism"), Franco's *Venus in Furs* explores the opposite side of S&M. This film is a thematic (rather than literal) adaption of the classic novel.

Venus in Furs is one of several of the director's films to feature the great Klaus Kinski. The movie also boasts performances from Dennis Price and Maria Rohm, both of whom also appeared in several of Franco's movies.

With *Venus in Furs*, the filmmaker approaches his material from a shifted dynamic viewpoint, looking at the sadomasochistic relationship through the masochist's eyes, rather than the sadist's, as is more often his wont.

A downtrodden trumpeter (James Darren)—in a stunning piece of slow-motion action combined with the right music—discovers a dead woman (Rohm) in the ocean and drags the body to shore. "She was beautiful, even if she was dead. There was a connection between us."

This scene segues into the story of the man's love affair with a ghost, and his quest for vengeance on the group of libertines responsible for her death. This vengeance, however, is revealed to be more the work of the ghost herself, though one can surmise that the energy and love of the living musician vivifies her.

There are some standout sequences in *Venus in Furs*. Scenes of reflection, for example, bring up memories where everyone is frozen in time, with only the trumpeter moving through a still tableau. Shots of Rio de Janeiro during Carnival are captivating, too.

Franco squeezed tons of production value into his low-budget films. For all the cruelty in the tale, this is also a lyrical movie. The director skillfully weaves together a distinct story with dreamy surrealism.

Venus in Furs is among Franco's more distinctive pieces of erotica. Its sexual dynamics are just slightly askew from his more "normal" erotic cinema, and it is a surprisingly heterosexual film for Franco. There is a more solid substrate of story under Manfred Mann's score of jazzy nervous tension.

The film is one of Franco's great classics. *Venus in Furs* is a rare balance in storytelling and experiential psychedelia. The film exhibits the director's skill in erotic presentation, but with a distinctive path. The cinematography is superb. Franco is in peak form here.

VENUS IN FURS

This is a swingin' movie and it swings as only Franco can.

An assault by flogging yanks us—and the trumpeter—abruptly into the S&M world populated by Kinski and his cronies (men and women both). It is attention-getting to see the members of this elite group, with their peculiar notions of pleasure, down on their hands and knees kissing and caressing a lusty flogged female, as though she were a carcass upon which the predators will feed.

The sequence is capped off by Kinski using a big, fancy knife to open a cut on the woman's shoulder, from which he sups.

Another memorable scene shows a woman in a bathtub, arms crossed over her chest as blood pools around her breasts and abdomen. She whispers dark words. There is a sturdy linearity to the story structure of *Venus in Furs*, as I mentioned above—but I never said it did not have an elliptical nature.

Venus in Furs ultimately circles back around to its beginning. This is a case where the surrealist component, rather than a transcendent plot, actually serves the story.

And at the center of this story is the trumpeter. Although he is swept

about by events and is something of a passive character, his emotional arc is an important part of the film.

Amidst the sex and violence the film has heart. Scenes of the musician playing on stage reveal a startlingly quiet sadness. And rather than standing out tonally from the psychedelic bizarreness playing out here, the trumpeter's melancholy is an organic ingredient of *Venus in Furs*.

Only a filmmaker like Jess Franco could have accomplished such a paradoxical piece of cinema. His low-budget but lavish style takes a singular form here, and the fact that this style is driven by a strong emotional current makes it an even stronger film.

BLUE RITA (1977)

Franco goes espionage and this is not the only time. But this was how he did it for 1977's *Blue Rita*. This film is one of the director's less known works, even for an artist well outside the mainstream already. There are more obscure works than even this one, but *Blue Rita* is far from the first title to come up in a discussion of the man's canon.

But it is also one of his most distinctive films.

Its titular character is Blue Rita (Martine Fléty, aka Karine Martin), an undercover spy who has the greatest cover story ever. She is a strip club owner and is herself a dancer when, you know, she isn't busy being James Bond with boobs.

The visuals are quite strange, even for Franco. They are what *Diabolique Magazine* called the movie's "sometimes bizarre modernist production design." *Blue Rita* achieves a tone of psychedelic mesmerism from the beginning. Franco's visual scheme and the superbly selected music, melded with the visuals, put us into a heightened state of immediate awareness.

Rita and her dancers—and her secret spies—employ severe techniques of sexual interrogation on their male targets. This is a brilliant plot point for the director's delivery of some psychosexuality, Franco style.

Blue Rita is a unique frolic that does not entirely align with his other work. This is one of his movies that is so original—both in terms of style and story/genre—that the film (despite its relative obscurity) draws attention to itself even within the context of Jess Franco's other films.

This movie is also a surprisingly alluring piece, loaded with a sense of fun. Indeed, the film displays a potent comedic tone in several places. Its farcical nature also contains an element of parody as it takes the spy genre to places where nobody else would have thought to steer it.

Of course there is the expected sexuality. Topless female spies in knee-high silver boots are pretty grabbing. Cock-teasing and the cultivation of blue balls are acceptable tools in these ladies' interrogation techniques. Nor are they above good ol' pain-based torture, such as pouring some apparently corrosive or acidic thick green liquid onto their victims. This green glop also induces maddening arousal in the male interrogation victim.

The tongue-in-cheek supertech devices and slow-death machinery are awesome low-rent references to the cheap sci-fi machinery used in old science fiction movies, as well as recalling the badass tech that the Bond villains were so good at obtaining and employing with diabolical glee.

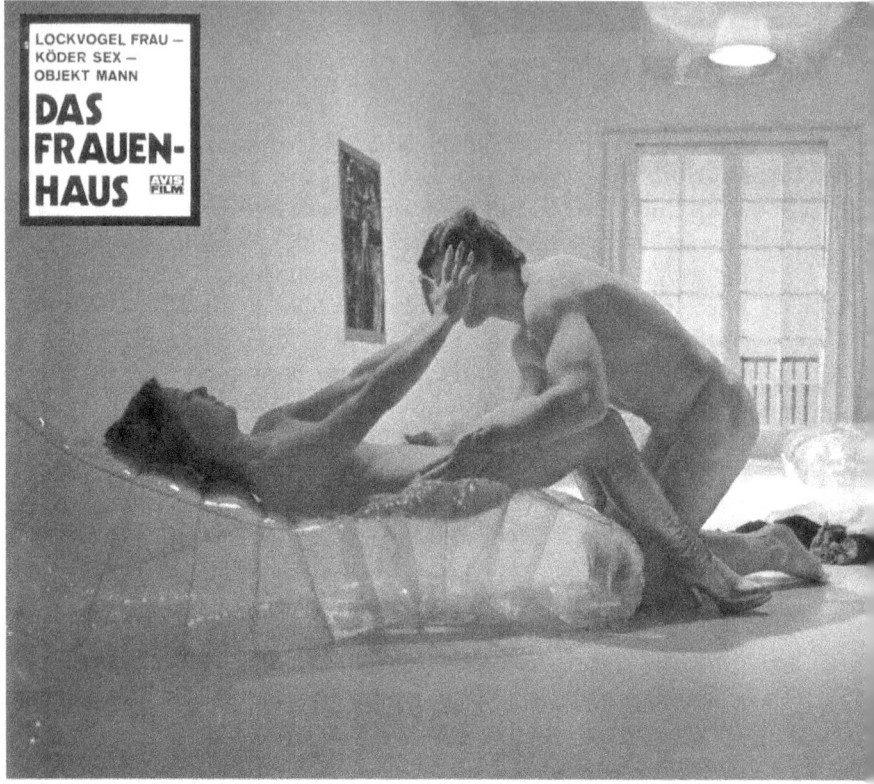

It is in scenes like this where the movie shows its satirical tone. *Blue Rita*, on one hand, can be seen as an erotic parody of the porno parodies of mainstream films. Soft core knockoffs of popular movies are far from a new concept in sex cinema. Here, Franco is crafting his own self-aware nod/prod at those, as well as poking fun at the original genre. He also pokes a stick at broader ideas, such as supposed media impartiality.

Plus, if you have never seen a woman, painted silver and wearing a decorative elephant mask over her head, then here is your chance to scratch it off your bucket list. It's all part of a bizarre, avant-garde live erotic show—an idea Franco hits on in other films.

Metatexual levels are created here, in that Franco's film is a bizarre erotic show containing within its reality another bizarre erotic show. Franco's world of cinema is loaded with subtext.

THE BLOODY JUDGE (1970)

Nobody—not a damn soul—can deny that Christopher Lee makes a thoroughly intimidating Inquisitor. In *The Bloody Judge*, he is, in fact, portraying a fictionalized version of the notorious witchfinder of the 1600s, Judge George Jeffreys. In this movie Franco touches on the dangers of excess zeal—whether religious or secular—as he also does in *The Demons*.

Interestingly, in some ways this is one of Franco's more "cinematic" films. It has a grandiosity and flourish that reminds one of the more familiar theatrical style of the classic theatrical epic. Yet, this is still a Franco film from beginning to the end.

Franco's mastery of challenging erotica and his beautiful eye for cinematography render this movie about a greatly cruel human being of the Inquisition, an era defined by its cruelty, an exercise in beauty even as it portrays an unflinching study of the darkest depravities of a person's soul.

Every human has a shadow side. Our inner shadow isn't entirely bad. Often shadow is just that—shadow, inner truths secreted away, often due to societal shame. But sometimes shadow is "evil." We all have the capacity for evil inside us. Some of us are pushed there more easily than others, but evil is a universal human trait. Our shadow, overall, is just our dark side, "dark" not to be automatically equated with "bad" or "evil." But there is a deep corner of our shadow where the foul things of which we all are capable reside.

The bloody judge isn't us ... but he could be.

This film is a quality production in a subgenre of horror not really known for quality, per se. Franco hides brilliant art in plain sight, but it hides behind sublime subversion and esoteric erotica easily misinterpreted by the uninitiated as sleaze. Sadly, obscure and mainstream cinema alike are too frequently the subject of shallow artistic analysis. Often this shallow analysis is a matter of film snobbery and the false hierarchies of genre significance.

The Bloody Judge is a classy film about sleazy people and heinous acts. And while we do thrill in our shadow at heady combinations like sex and torture, Franco's expert addressing of the subject reminds us that it is simply a part of us to have morbid interests. Thanatos is, after all, a driving force in the heart and mind of man. Plus, we all have our dark—and our too-dark—sides. So the film tells us to be okay with our shadow, but to beware of its deepest regions—without failing to acknowledge them.

There are some uncomfortable torture sequences, which serve to simultaneously titillate and disturb us. Exactly the sort of thing at which Franco excels. He ever loves to challenge us.

Aside from being a religious satire, *The Bloody Judge* examines the deadly dangers of authority—and too much of it—in particular. What is true of the Inquisition is also true, to varying degrees, of governments. For that matter, the Roman Catholic Church *was* effectively the government at the time of the Inquisition. It is a terrible truth that government, which in theory is supposed to concern itself with its citizens' welfare, is far too susceptible to human ego.

Power is heady and leads to all kinds of offenses and atrocities.

I doubt Franco meant it as such, but I like to pretend that this film is a libertarian statement. At the very least, the idea is there, even if of its own spontaneity. Which is fine by me.

Classic liberalism has as one of its pillars the doctrine of spontaneous order, such as would be manifest in any true capitalist system (not to be confused with the government-abetting corporate cronyism that is always wrongly labeled as an example of capitalism). But I digress.

Of course, a film like *The Bloody Judge* is about paranoia, too, if not in the same way as John Carpenter's *The Thing*, which is *the* modern cinematic statement on paranoia. Carpenter's movie is an intense tale of paranoia on a small but volatile scale, in a situation that is claustrophobic on the inside by dint of the agoraphobia of snow white waiting on the outside. Franco's *Judge*, however, is a broader look at paranoia in the heart of man, particularly where true-believer idealism is involved, with the Inquisition providing the setting for examining these themes.

Paranoia is a domino effect in which the social organism eventually devours itself. This film features the compelling touch that even the cold-blooded judge of inquisitional infamy is haunted in his dreams, at the depth of his soul, by the atrocities for which he is responsible. It is a question: Can even most foul and corrupt of men be aware of their guilt—all ideals aside—in the long night, deep in the soul?

The inclusion of a subplot about star-crossed lovers separated by the vile Inquisition's habitually wrong accusations brings an added poignancy to the proceedings. This subplot prevents the film's themes from being expressed as merely a universal abstract. The lovers' fate personalizes the injustice inherent in the Inquisition, providing a poignancy that makes the film far more affecting.

Basically, the innocents sought out as witches represent the outside-the-box, truly progressive and open-minded thinkers in society and the

threat they pose to the bell curve hump and the dominant mediocre mind. We therefore also witness the consequent unnecessary paranoia-inducing fear induced in the hearts of the status quo who wish to see no rocking of the boat. From this fear they derive a false sense of doom at what might happen with a paradigm shift. They are unaware that there is nothing but change, at least at this human level of perception.

MANSION OF THE LIVING DEAD (1982)

This movie is a tribute to Amando de Ossorio's *Blind Dead* tetralogy of films. *Mansion of the Living Dead* is also one of my favorite zombie movies, while being so much more than a mere zombie movie. I think that most of my favorite zombie movies (an elite handful given that I don't like zombie movies, as a rule) are those in which Franco had a hand. I also must say that I like *Mansion of the Living Dead* much more than the de Ossorio series.

The film, after an uber-moody opening, commences with the seemingly mundane story of four women on vacation and out for some fun. But a surrealist element inserts itself as we begin to realize that their checking into the hotel signifies a crossing over to a supernatural, parallel reality.

It bears repeating that *Mansion of the Living Dead* is more than just a zombie film. Zombies do not become a major factor until later in the picture. There is also a mysterious subplot involving a woman chained to a wall in one of the rooms of the hotel, a hotel that seems to be empty but for the four girls, the captive woman and the handsome young man running the hotel.

Mansion of the Living Dead is one of Franco's more minimalist films, while being visually absorbing and laced with generous helpings of atmosphere. This film is a terrific example of Franco using one of his innate skills: creating stunning form with a spartan budget. Franco has accomplished this feat many times, but *Mansion of the Living Dead* seems a particularly strong example. The film's relatively understated aesthetic and dense mood, here applied subtly, are outstanding in their nuanced crafting of the film's aura.

The intense mood of the film takes full hold with the appearance of the zombie monks in the film's second half. We also move into subtextual territory that is similar to Franco's Inquisition movies. The zombie monks in *Mansion* are effectively prudish, moralistic minded religious punishers—from beyond the grave. As is evident in Franco's Inquisition movies, these dastardly zombies—who are interested in something more than ordinary gut munching—employ evil to punish perceived evil.

The Inquisition zealots of history had their torture racks. The zombie monks in *Mansion of the Living Dead* rape and ritually sacrifice women guilty of promiscuity and hedonism. So ... fight fire with fire? We have the same satirical statement as that present in *The Demons* or

The Bloody Judge, only with a different fictional vehicle, albeit one that reveals tight parallels to the Inquisition movies.

Hell, these zombies even pray for forgiveness for their own knowingly committed sins (you know, rape and murder and the like), a situation reminiscent of Ingmar Bergman's *The Virgin Spring*, when the father of the murdered girl does preemptory penance for the revenge murders he and his family are on the brink of committing. The difference between the two movies lies in the tone and intent of the two directors. Bergman's proactive forgiveness begging is sincere and therefore lacks much of the sharp satirical irony that Franco intends with his nasty, praying walking-dead monks.

The physical corruption of the undead monks is of course a manifestation of their inner corruption.

One of my favorite sequences in this film is when the ladies go to the beach for some topless sunbathing only to have a MEAT CLEAVER thrown by some crazy kook embed itself in the sand near them. This scene forms a curious sequence, and one—I can't elucidate on why I feel this way—that without which the film would be somehow incomplete.

Mansion of the Living Dead is probably one of the most original zombie movies you are apt to encounter. The layered stacking of eclectic horror themes provides a textured approach to the realm of the undead on film. One of its layers is Franco's surprisingly organic application of sadism to the zombie genre in its multiple forms and the seamless positioning within the movie of non-zombie themes.

One example is when (before we ever see the cruel punishment meted out to the women by the zombie monks) we are alerted to the existence of a woman chained up by a metal leash in her hotel room. She has a love-hate thing going with her captor that includes a deviant version of the Stockholm Syndrome. This scene moves way beyond conventional undead fare.

And we have the zombie monks themselves, who really start going full-tilt-walking-dead-Inquisition right around the halfway mark of the movie. Here we have something that Franco does well with his zombies: he uses very simple makeup that nevertheless ranges from quietly effective to visually striking. As in Andrea Bianchi's *Burial Ground: Nights of Terror* or Franco's own *Oasis of the Zombies*, the zombie makeup seen in *Mansion of the Living Dead* is not high-tech, but is, regardless, very effective despite its simplicity.

Like *Oasis of the Zombies*, this is a one-of-a-kind zombie picture and as you can tell a favorite of mine.

LOVE LETTERS OF A PORTUGUESE NUN (1977)

So how about a nunsploitation film gone art house via Jess Franco that tells the tale of a girl who is compelled to join a convent that is, behind the scenes, controlled by Satanists? That is, in fact, the plot of this curiously titled Franco film. This isn't one of his more well-known pictures, but worthy of mention here, nonetheless.

The usual subtexts about authority and cruelty are present, as would be expected. But this film approaches us at a slightly different angle from other films in the nun-horror genre, story-wise at least. Untypically, the girl's behavior in this film is less than saintly. Still, however, her behavior is hardly evil; she is simply as unconcerned with traditional moral conventions as is Franco himself. God forbid the girl acts like a human being!

To add insult to injury for the mother whose daughter must enter a convent to save her soul, the representative of the church who insists on the girl's isolation from society also demands a dowry. In this case, the insistent clergyman, who also runs the convent into which he is placing the girl, makes off with the mother's savings.

All done in the name of God, of course. And to rub salt into the wound: should the mother fail to pay the convent, she will be declared co-responsible for her daughter's sins and will end up in purgatory while her daughter, presumably, burns in hell. This is a cutting statement on the use of fear to control people. The threat of the wrath of God kept the Roman Catholic Church in power for too many centuries. Terrorism has served the United States well.

There are parallels here with the WIP genre, in that we have a group of females—nuns rather than inmates—in thrall to a cruel female authority. One scene has the mother superior performing an invasive test of the newly arrived girl's claim to virginity; this barbarity is enacted in front of other nuns. A confession scene has a priest salaciously teasing out every possible detail of sexual sin from the girl. These scenes are an in-your-face expression of moral hypocrisy, as well as articulating Franco's recurring theme of mislabeled good and evil. The innocent girl is declared unrighteous and bedeviled by a supposedly holy priest who fully relishes all the "sinful" confessional details. This sick perversion of holy confession later leads to a much more direct sensual encounter between priest and nun.

Broadly speaking, the film is about the corruption lying behind apparent wholesomeness. David Lynch's *Blue Velvet* struck the same

chord using suburbia, rather than religion, and its picket fence false front for exposing the dirty underbelly of society.

Love Letters of a Portuguese Nun is an atmospheric and beautifully shot movie laden with satire about hypocrisy and meanness in the name of a false morality. Two women enjoying each other erotically is loudly proclaimed as sin, but the true sins are committed with the tyrannical knee-jerk reactions of the deceitful head figures populating this Satanic cult disguised as a home for the servants of God. The most fervent self-proclaimed moralists are the greatest sinners. This portrayal of Satanism masquerading as Christianity is a heady statement on moral hypocrisy.

This nasty fictionalized Satanism asserts itself rather harshly during a scene in which a secretly satanic nun speaks of the healing poultice made from a baby's heart. The heart is not shown, but the very idea, coupled with a moaning nun ... well, that is going to leave a mental scar. This is an intense Eros-Thanatos scene. So too are the shots of hairy, clawed hands raking a bloody path across a naked female body. Medieval torture devices also add to the menace.

The girl's gauntlet of introduction into the depravity of this corrupt convent escalates to her having sex with the Dark Lord himself, an event which cannot help but recall the film *Rosemary's Baby* from Ira Levin and Roman Polanski.

We also observe a shameless bacchanalia, an orgy of nuns. Pure, energized eroticism in the name of God, in the name of Satan. Blasphemy, once you get high enough in the organization, apparently, is quite overt in these hedonic rituals. The subtext: leading the girl to holiness actually leads to corruption and false ideals. But when she confronts her superior about the satanic ritual, she is told that she must have dreamed or hallucinated the whole thing. So the acts by which she, an innocent, is drawn into through deceit of the highest order, are turned upon her, used against her and attributed to her own corrupt nature—rather than her tormentors revealing that these acts are the result of a corruption festering in servants of Satan masquerading as agents of God.

This is a cutting statement on the reactionary tendency to condemn anything resembling a real question.

Bucking the system and seeking help only lands the woman in further inquisitional bondage. Bad things are in store. Franco depicts the use of dire fear, again, as a tool for oppression. In fear for their own fate, should their secret Satanism be discovered by the Inquisition, the leaders of the convent—filthy priest and corrupt mother superior—instead turn the implements of torture they deserve upon an innocent who warrants no such cruel infliction of pain and bodily damage.

Moral: the powers that be will do anything to shut you up.

ATTACK OF THE ROBOTS (1966)

Attack of the Robots is a fresh—if old—manifestation of Francoan filmmaking. This movie is a mondo mash-up of espionage and sci-fi shot early in his career. Franco already had a couple of Dr. Orloff flicks under his belt, and a smattering of other films, but this movie seems way out for him, even back then.

Hell, this film even feels way out for the filmmaker by today's standards. But at least we now have the luxury of appraising the majority of his canon; remember, nobody for sure knows how many Jess Franco films there are and many of them are not readily available. This film has a buzzing sense of pure fun, while it still also offers a bit of the rough grit to be had in a tough action-espionage feature.

Add the super-villainous sci-fi element—how does a man turn colors like that when he mysteriously dies?—and you have a dandy, eccentric film that feels like a gonzo resurrection of the classic serials and Saturday matinee B-movie sci-fi/horror/action fare.

The movie really does have some of the sensation of being Agent 007 James Bond meets the Saturday matinee serial, but fused by Jess Franco into a whole distinctly marked with this filmmaker's signature style. No matter how that style may evolve from film to film, it remains always Franco. It is always a pleasure to see Franco find these tangents and then totally make them his own.

Even in a fun-time romp like this, Franco does not skimp on quality visual expression, and as I have said aplenty, I am always fond of seeing the director work in black-and-white.

Anyone who thinks that they have seen everything gonzo filmmaker Jess Franco has to offer needs to seek out *Attack of the Robots* for a singular Francoan experience that is also a wonderful throwback to classic B cinema. Every time you think you know how versatile Jess Franco was as a filmmaker, along comes another film to challenge this assertion.

While this film isn't anywhere near being one of Franco's hyper-erotic works, he still can't leave sex appeal out of *Attack of the Robots*. There are clothed but hypnotically alluring femme fatales in this movie that you will also discover in any number of noir and espionage stories. In *Attack of the Robots* we find threads of both noir and espionage.

On a side note: I would like to point out that Franco's famous zoom lens makes a brief appearance or two in *Attack of the Robots*. I find it interesting how everything that makes Franco tick as a filmmaker has some obvious germinal roots in his early material. Franco, as we know him, was always there from the beginning, even in a kid-friendly sci-spy movie like the director's little known *Attack of the Robots*.

THE EROTIC RITES OF FRANKENSTEIN (1972)

This movie is a sister act to *Dracula, Prisoner of Frankenstein*, also released in 1972 and is even more of a gonzo mondo monsters run amok flick than its cinematic sibling. *Dracula, Prisoner of Frankenstein* is also, by comparison, more low key than *The Erotic Rites of Frankenstein*.

Franco made more than one homage to classic monster fare (think old-school Universal Pictures) at this time in his career, and this is among the more gonzo of the group. This film is a complete revamp *à la* Franco and lends forward-thinking movement to the development of classic horror movie themes.

The Erotic Rites of Frankenstein is a bit more over the top among Franco's monster mashers, and I mean that in the best possible way. This review is plainly a laud from me to Franco, an homage to the filmmaker's astounding capacity for taking what essentially would be low rent camp fodder in another filmmaker's hand, and turning it into hyperbolic guerilla art.

One of the characters I suspect the unprepared would be quick to dismiss as idiotically campy is the bird woman, played by Anne Libert. Sure, her costume is simple and the echoing bird noises she emits are startling, but this character is actually a pretty original way to present an animal-human beast. Dr. Moreau would be proud.

Franco has never veered away from using low-tech, non-realistic and non-representative (in terms of verisimilitude) methods to convey his artfully insane ideas. Why should this film be any different? Franco is a challenging director, even if he is challenging you with one of his several monster movie homages to the classic vintage creature features.

Even when creating a pastiche, Franco makes the material his own. His method of ever shaping his films, regardless of content, into a creation of his own, is something I truly admire in the now deceased director. He blends several iconic monster stories by including revisionist characters based upon the originals: Doctor Seward, Dr. Frankenstein (Franco regular Dennis Price), Cagliostro (another regular, Howard Vernon), plus, of course, the Frankenstein monster.

I sadly lament that I never did have the chance to speak to the art house auteur genius who was the singular, utterly unique Jess Franco.

I suppose that, in a way, this book is an extended love letter and an ode to a cinematic master and an artist of sharp originality, regardless of which medium he chose to use.

No creator was like him, be they author, singer, painter, filmmaker or aught else. This clearly is not to say that other artists are not his equals, or even superiors in some cases (whatever such subjectivity really means in an artistic context), but I assert, without hesitation, that Franco is absolutely and unquestionably a phenomenon entirely unto himself.

He may have peers of artistic greatness (and he most certainly does) but none of them are like him and he is not like any of them, either.

One-of-a-kind means just exactly that.

The Erotic Rites of Frankenstein, however Franco-gonzo it might be, never once loses sight of the fact that it is a tribute to the old school monsters of eras past—monsters that still fascinate us and almost certainly always will.

Frankensteinian creations will always and forever represent the shaking of one's fist in the face of God, or at least they perennially reflect man's fear of what may be transgressive in science.

The bird woman (Anne Libert) touches on the tension inherent in the false idea that we and the animals are separate.

She mocks the mindset that says we are not animals, even though we are. The hypocrisy lies in the rejection/fear of the primal in us, the reptilian brain, pure instinctual drives that do not have anything to do with prescribed morality and socio-cultural restraint. The bird woman is beyond the concept of the transcendent ubermensch, although she presumably embraces the fullness of human nature, or at least acknowledges and comes to terms with it in all its various and sundry facets. The attitude of denying our basic animal nature is in fact regressive, rather than progressive.

We may have grown a veneer of civilization around our purely animalistic selves (which typically hides in our inward shadow, where things are "safe" in their secretness, out of sight and mind), but that side of us undeniably remains. We have a tincture of Sir William Golding's *Lord of the Flies* here among the monsters.

As my sociology teacher in high school said of Golding's book, all you have to do is scratch at the surface a little to see how thin the veneer of civilization actually is. The right or wrong situation—however you prefer to look at it—can create a place in which all the ethical constructs of society fade away and we return to the state of "might makes right."

Not that we ever left that state, our primitive self is just more cleverly well hidden today. Under that veneer.

Think about it. Does a government have an inherent natural authority over you? Or is a government in charge because it has the power and the *fire*power?

These are things worth considering and are part of the dynamics tucked away in Franco's *The Erotic Rites of Frankenstein.*

It is probably stating the obvious that this movie also allows Franco the chance to exercise his gothic filmmaking skills. I have established that gothic cinema is a strength of Franco's. His transgressiveness is apparent in the scene in which a naked man and woman are tied together upon a spiked platform—don't fall down and be sure to watch *Flash Gordon* when it comes out about eight years after this.

Meanwhile, grit your teeth and endure the flogging. I say that because Frankenstein's monster—silver-skinned in this incarnation—is flailing the shit out of the hapless pair with a whip.

The titular monster in *The Erotic Rites of Frankenstein.*

The Erotic Rites of Frankenstein is a delirious reworking of old monster movie material, and this film is the kind of retooling only someone the likes of Jess Franco could have accomplished. The director sometimes likes to spring a blend of that which is classic with his particular sense of subversive progressiveness—and it is pretty much always a reward for the viewer whenever Franco does this.

THE SEX IS CRAZY (1981)

With this film, Franco dabbles in erotic sci-fi parody. He is forever stretching himself, as I keep emphasizing.

This tongue-in-cheek sexy sci-fi foray *The Sex is Crazy* is most definitely among the director's lesser known movies and I wish that it had more of an audience than it does.

The crazy story involves women who work as actresses in science-fiction porno movies. But life wackily starts to imitate art when these ladies are beset by sex-hungry aliens. There seems to be some kind of procreation problem for the aliens, so they have come to bang some humans.

This is the plot of a kooky porno movie where actresses in kooky porno movies end up in actual kooky situations that parallel their movie lives. The meta here is deceptively obvious.

This film could be misinterpreted as a silly porn flick at the drop of a hat, but its layered satire actually parodies such movies by disguising itself as one.

One of Franco's favored techniques is to start with something horrific, transgressively erotic or, in this case, sexually graphic sci-fi, only to reveal that a scene is actually part of some bizarre theater show enjoyed by an audience that clearly likes its avant-garde entertainment.

Such is the case here, and with the invasion of the highly libidinous extra-terrestrials the scene morphs into an alien-themed sex show.

It's groovy as hell that Franco is able to work subtext into a seemingly trite (but not really) example of comedic sexy sci-fi satire cinema. There is even some mystery intrigue worked into the story.

This is a weird one, which obviously could be said of most any Franco movie, but really, this is a weird one.

Even amongst all the nuttiness, Franco is more than able to conjure atmosphere. He is a director who, if he wants to, is going to do it and do it well. Despite the movie's uber-low budget and quirky conceits, his work is more effective than it probably has any right to be.

Franco even manages to use rubber monster masks for some of his creepy characters, but he *still* makes this hokey ploy work. The ultra-simple technique of employing rubber masks actually elevates the creep factor.

The Sex is Crazy is not only an obvious stab at whacky plots in porn movies and such, but the movie is also a hilarious, over-the-top, erotically themed, micro-budget science-fiction flick that reveals paradoxical slabs of ominous mood during its key scenes.

The director's ability to work within a low budget, spartan sets, etc. while still making *his* movie, is certainly evident in this slice of cinematic strangeness. Minimalism is an effective component of the film's mien and helps make the movie work.

ILSA THE WICKED WARDEN (1977)

Ilsa is perhaps one of the most feared names in Women in Prison (WIP) cinema, the ultimate archetype of the evil warden bitch who takes a sick delight in the horrible tortures she inflicts upon her female inmates.

Dyanne Thorne has earned some serious genre movie fame playing the cruel mistress of other women, a despotic female prison warden who relishes her power over these inmate women, applying her power in a most sadistic manner. Nothing is too dreadful to inflict upon the captive women under her diabolical administration.

Thorne, in fact, portrayed the evil bitch jail boss—who acts more like a dominatrix than a prison administrator—in four different Ilsa movies. Ilsa is arguably the character for which she is best known, although the actress has done other work in a variety of films and genres. She is probably best known to fans of horror and related genres, particularly the women-in-prison genre.

This film also features sexy Lina Romay, who assumed the role of Franco's muse following the tragic death of Soledad Miranda.

Ilsa the Wicked Warden introduces some major elements of the WIP film without delay. A bevy of naked beauties get all cleaned up together in the inmates' prison shower. Such *en masse* nudity is perfect material for a master of the erotic such as Jess Franco. The scene lays the ground work for one of his favored themes, the fusion of sex and violence or death.

Eros and Thanatos.

The movie's early sequences also feature a harrowing escape attempt into the jungle surrounding this remote and brutal prison. This is a prison designed to hold not only criminal inmates of the female persuasion, but also rather a more specialized type of "deviant" prisoner. This prison is a prison hospital. The inmates are "patients."

These are women who have one kind of mental disorder or another and they are presumably guilty of some action associated with their mental illness that has landed them in this prison "clinic". That is, if you consider something like lesbianism to be a mental disorder.

Nymphomania is also cited in *Ilsa the Wicked Warden* as a justifiable lock-up offense. Are the nymphos in this high security clinic/jail/hellhole a particularly onerous or aggressive variety—possessing a horniness so aggressive that it constitutes assault?

Of course, nymphomania is considered a mental disorder according

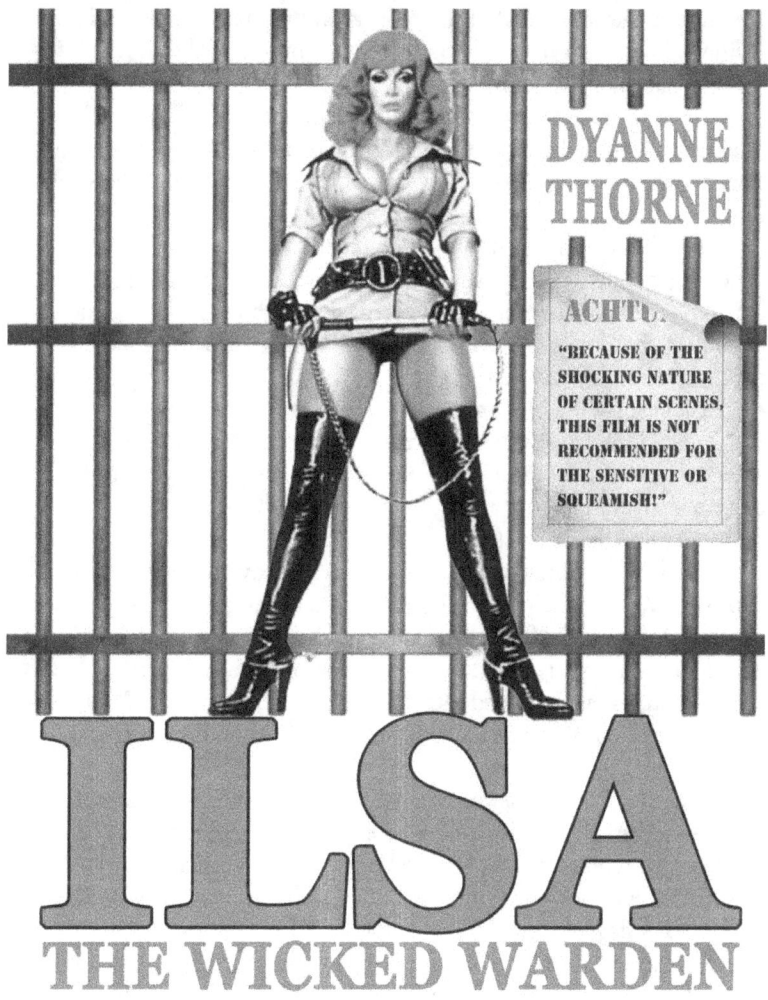

to the Diagnostic Statistical Manual (the bible of psychiatry) and nymphomania can be a self-destructive behavior. But I do not believe that the dehumanizing punishment dispensed by psycho warden Dyanne Thorne is a suitable cure for the disease.

Topics such as these highlight the theme of the fear and repression of female sexuality. The irony here is that we see another woman punishing the victimized female inmates of the jail. There is no male patriarch applying the abuse, as we see in Franco's nunsploitation films.

Still, it is suggested here that the repression of female power and the divine feminine is a distinctly patriarchal effort.

However, there are many women deluded into accepting a secondary position in the natural, social and divine orders as established in unbreakable stone by a deity with a real chauvinist streak. So Dyanne Thorne could be a symbol analogous to the stereotypical/archetypal mean old nun.

(Watch that knuckle-slapping ruler, dig?)

More generally we are also visiting—as we do so often in Franco's cinema—the broader theme of the capacity for human cruelty and vicious lusting for power lying in every human breast, be it merely potential or fully activated.

A fearful suspense plot ensues when a woman whose sister disappeared into this wicked correctional system demands that she be admitted to the prison for a month—under false pretenses—so that she can poke around and try to dig up some information on what might have happened to her sister.

A doctor whom she convinces to help is already trying to mount a campaign against the prison, despite the fact that authorities (as always) do not see sufficient reason to go barging into the, uh, clinic for any reason that is based only upon rumors and whispers. The fact that nobody is ever allowed into the prison and that none of the patients are allowed out ensures that there are little more than vague, quiet hints of wrongdoing.

Ilsa the Wicked Warden also delves into another Franco-favored theme—sadism, be it with willing, compliant masochists or, as here, with people who have little choice but to endure such abuse. The first disturbing but compelling appearance of sadistic behavior is when the evil warden has her favorite inmate lie naked on the warden's bed, after having received a massage from a woman whose life as an inmate is better for being the teacher's pet—better being a relative term.

Then, the warden, one by one, inserts needles into the inmate's chest between her breasts. After administering these tiny, quiet pricks of sado-pain (resembling some unholy act of acupuncture), the warden suddenly lies down across the naked inmate and embraces her—which has the effect (unseen yet vivid in the mind's eye) of pressing the needles deeper into the victimized woman's chest.

While the inmate is technically a willing participant—she does get special privileges in return for playing spy for Ilsa and for other services rendered as just described above—it isn't as though she has much choice. She can either act willing, going with the flow of the wicked warden's evil Tao—or she can resist and suffer worse punishment and also lose the few extra perks she receives for her cooperation.

Such singling out for attention also creates an extra layer in the prison hierarchy. As the warden's favorite lady inmate, she is tacitly awarded a slightly elevated status. So much so that she feels comfortable demanding that the new girl, the sister seeker, scrub her back—and other, more delicate parts. When the new inmate balks at scrubbing anything more than a back, the warden's pet is sufficiently offended to feel totally justified in starting a naked shower catfight over the disrespect shown by the new girl, who is naturally lowest on the totem pole anyway.

The extra layer of hierarchy, rather than being simply inmates and warden, is actually inmates, then one special inmate, then the warden. This extra layer creates more layers of conflict, as well. For example, a government can help keep its power intact by creating and maintaining a schism amongst the citizenry—who might otherwise unite and cast a vengeful eye on the government it hates and distrusts. Keep the people divided and your own power is enhanced and stabilized.

The pretend inmate on a mission becomes a victim of the situation and is punished by Ilsa. As with the needle sequence during which we see only the lightest foreplay aspects of the torture (just the initial acupuncture), Franco's restraint here keeps a subsequent heinous event that happens during this punishment out of sight but for a puff of smoke.

This is a gut-twister of a scene. A heated metal device, cylindrical and with a pointed tip, is applied to the poor woman's vagina. That smoke puff and the imagining of what was done creates a terrible mental image coiling into a fascinated disgust in one's belly and stays in one's mind long after.

The application of electrodes to the temples of the inmate—who by now no doubt wishes she hadn't wormed her way into the clinic from hell—seems minor in comparison, although in its own right this torture is bad enough as it inflicts psychological pain and well as physical pain.

Just as the electricity is unseen but the suggestion of its presence via the sight of the electrodes causes us to flinch at what we can "feel" but not see, so too does the unseen genital mutilation—depicted visually with only the smoke (which also conjures in my mind the sense of an awful burning stench)—creates its impact by suggestion and not with explicitness.

And again, this burning awfulness creates not only physical horror but also psychological horror. Genital mutilation is one of the most rotten things one can imagine in terms of physical maiming. Not only is genital mutilation an ultra-invasive physical act, but this abomination also threatens the part of our identity (attached to our physicality and gender) that is a defining trait of who we are as human beings. The unrestrained cruelty of this act, coupled with the surrounding atmosphere of prison hopelessness, makes this one of genre cinema's most horrifying scenes.

It is bad enough to be stripped of one's name and be known only as a number, but to have one's identity violated so invasively is beyond hell.

The new girl—who, by the way, is shuttled off to the isolation cell after her devastating punishment—can expect things to just keep getting worse. Once Ilsa learns that the newbie has been asking around about the missing woman, it becomes the warden's top concern to find out who this new inmate is and why she is making inquiries.

The bosses of these torture prisons are always worried that word will get out that normal prison regulations regarding a prisoner merely serving time or participating in healthy rehabilitation programs have been jettisoned and replaced by more ... forceful ... techniques. Worse, what will happen if people learn that these "progressive, advanced new techniques" for curing a patient or rehabilitating a criminal are a camouflage for pure, malevolent abuse of power with no other end but the torture of helpless souls and the sick gratification of the torturers' egos?

Things get really scary when the new inmate, subject to heinous torture, divulges information that allows Ilsa to discover the identity of the doctor who had the sister-seeker committed. The warden sends a couple of uniformed thugs to take care of the problem, by which I mean to shoot the doctor in his face and then bury his body.

Now, the woman who simply wanted to discover the fate of her missing sibling is stuck behind bars and the only person who knew the truth about her real identity is dead and beyond helping her.

Wrongful imprisonment or commitment—when no one knows that you are innocent—is one of the most terrifying dilemmas I can imagine. The disturbing possibility of it ever happening to you ties a tight Gordian knot in your guts when you contemplate the potential outcomes. The fascination of this scenario has drawn Franco (as well as other filmmakers) to explore its dramatic possibilities.

SHE KILLED IN ECSTASY (1970)

This film is truly classic Franco. It is chock full of revenge, sex, non-traditional science and medicine, challenges to the status quo and metaphysical ponderings. I would say that this is among Franco's more important films. Despite the fact that the film is rife with recurring Franco themes, *She Killed in Ecstasy* also holds a unique position among the director's films as we shall see.

A beautiful woman (the luscious Soledad Miranda) suffers through the suicide of her husband, a doctor whose colleagues rejected his

unorthodox research. This rejection leads to his despondency and suicide. The blow of his suicide is too much for the young wife to bear, spawning a hatred for those she believes are responsible and inspiring a series of revenge murders.

The opening scene immediately impresses us with Franco's impeccable eye for cinematography and composition. The beauty of this scene engages our attention even before the intriguing plot and premise of *She Killed in Ecstasy* really gets rolling.

The woman's husband could be interpreted as the archetypal mad doctor shunned for his scientific blasphemies. But I prefer an alternate interpretation. As shocking as his ideas are, the film seems inclined to see him in favorable terms. He is presented as a kind, humane doctor whose ideas are simply too revolutionary for mainstream science.

In that context, we can readily feel sympathy for the wife and fully appreciate her rage—even if we would not go as far as she does to avenge his death.

The woman is so consumed by revenge-seeking that she is not above using her own riveting sexuality and beauty to lure her male victims to their doom. She entices them to bed where she reverses the normal male/female penetration relationship—they seek to enter her during sexual union, but she impales their bodies with her blade instead.

Well, that is the case in at least one of the murders. The reversed phallic dynamic, representative of the vindictive woman's general overturning of the orthodox male-dominated sex power structure, is worth note. Especially as it occurs during the inaugural murder. (A scissor kill seen later in the film carries the same effect and subtextual concept.)

Also, one of the doctors is a female, which adds a twist in the subtext and dynamics. And the execution of her murder is particularly visually striking. An inflatable pillow is used to suffocate the female doctor. Since portions of the pillow are transparent, we are able to see the breathless grimace of the victim's face as it is smashed against the pillow.

The scene includes a shot of the room—its white dominance highlighted by a couple of red objects—dramatizing the use of light and shadow and the framing of the shot—as well as the actual point of murder.

What a grabber of a shot!

Franco creates a dense singularity of sex and death pressed together, shaken together, and running over.

She Killed in Ecstasy is a somber film, despite its occasional high-energy jazz score and sexy murders. The film is a melancholic piece of

Soledad Miranda in *She Killed in Ecstasy.*

cinema that repeatedly returns to the mournful ruminations of the vengeful young woman. Her every prior purpose in life has been sublimated by her rage. Her only reason for living now, her only purpose, is the destruction of those who destroyed her by denying her the love of her life.

She has nothing left. Her only passion now is revenge, which is a twisted extension of her passion for her lost lover, with whom she desperately wants reunion.

This makes us wonder, quite naturally, if the last killing in the movie will be, not the killing of the last remaining doctor, but her own death. Her reason to live was her lover. With his death, the only remaining reason to stay alive that still provides her with a vital connection to her lover is the murder of those who drove him to suicide. She cannot of course bring him back to life from the dead. The best she can do is to destroy those who she believes are responsible for his death.

With the revenge motivation satiated, what other reason will this woman—tragically past an emotional point of no return—have to go on living? It is a question raised fairly early in the film when we hear the woman's thoughts: her desperate desire to see him again. This, coupled with the obvious eggs-in-one-basket focus of concentration on the desire for revenge, suggests to us that her connection to this world is tenuous.

This is the key thread of suspense running through *She Killed in Ecstasy*.

So desperate is her devotion to her lost lover that she keeps his body in bed the whole time she is out slaughtering her prey. Everything points to her being finished with this world once her crusade is complete. She no longer has an attachment to the realm of the living. Not anymore. Her only attachment now is to the man she loves from the opposite side of the veil.

The question is, will she, or will she not, decide to join him on the other side of the veil?

And all this assumes that she will successfully get away with murder. Multiple murders at that. So another question in the arc of suspense is whether her life is even in her own hands. She takes the lives of others into her hands, but there is no guarantee that her life will stay out of the reach of those who would stop her.

What she does at the end of the story is not quite what we expect. We expect her to turn her cutting-kill method on herself. But instead, she carefully arranges her dead lover next to her on the front seat of the car.

Then she drives off a cliff.

Rather than sending the vehicle into gravity's grasp with rocks below to merely dispose of a body, the woman is in essence performing a noble joint burial for two star-crossed lovers.

The film's closing lines are spoken by an authority at the crash site. At first they seem gratuitous and tacked on—but then one realizes there is a purpose behind the man's words. He explains that the hellbent-on-revenge lady, who in the end has also destroyed herself, was in fact, a perfectly normal person. If not for the devastation, despair and anger stemming from her lover's suicide, she would never have done anything like this.

This is a familiar Franco theme, so ubiquitous in the director's movies, that hides in plain sight, rather than roaring from the subtext. The theme is simply that the potential for mayhem is present in all our dark little hearts should the right trigger come along.

MARQUIS DE SADE'S JUSTINE (1969)

Justine is one of Franco's masterpieces of philosophical erotic transgression. This film is the director's interpretation of the novel *Justine, or The Misfortunes of Virtue* by the Marquis de Sade, a satire that tackled the idea that religious moral propriety doesn't guarantee you a damn thing.

At least not in this life. As the subtitle would suggest, the book is about the punishment of virtue rather than its reward. Faith does not mean the absence of tribulation, but rather the peaceful endurance of the evils life will hurl at us, sometimes without relent.

The word "sadism" is of course derived from the infamous author and libertine philosopher who spent ten years imprisoned in the notorious Bastille (where he continued to write the kind of stuff that got him locked away to begin with). Franco is a kindred spirit of de Sade: he is unafraid to confront head-on and without trepidation the concept of sadism as well as its philosophical and psychological implications.

Franco is equally lacking in fear, but uses the cinematic narrative as a tool for the artistic critique of corrupt and hypocritical power structures and moral codes, be they religious or otherwise.

This movie is also one of the filmmaker's unflinching examinations of the trauma caused by the loss of innocence. It is about the terror of enlightenment.

Justine features Klaus Kinski as the Marquis de Sade in a metatextual role that places the writer in his own story. Romina Power appears as Justine, and Maria Rohm plays Juliette, which is incidentally the name of a character in another de Sade novel.

Misfortune befalls Justine immediately once the movie gets the credits out of the way. We feel as if we are being warned that there is always trouble right around the corner if one isn't wary, regardless of how chipper you may be feeling right at the moment or how pleasant and benign the world and life may seem to you just then.

Stay vigilant, urges the story.

For Justine life becomes a complete and ruthless downhill tumble from the moment she leaves her safe and sheltered world. By extension, the movie warns us that a dangerous naïveté can be a bi-product arising from the strict application of a false, superficial morality.

Losing one's home in a convent is the *high point* of our heroine's misadventures. Justine's fortunes deteriorate horribly from this point

on. She descends into a wild, delirious world of extreme libertinism, experiencing all kinds of frightfully conceived modes of sexual sadism.

Justine's fate becomes worse after worse after worse. She falls into her very own circle of hell despite her powerful faith. A scary introduction to harsh reality violates the previous innocence of young Justine. Her chastity and ignorance of evil rival even that of Eve, of Garden of Eden renown, before Eve's verboten munching of the apple. The consumption of that fruit has become archetypically symbolic of the loss of innocence and its consequent shock of self-awareness. Such is the significance of the Tree of the Knowledge and Good and Evil.

Man's fate is the story of enlightenment recounted in Genesis as told by the medium of sacred writ. Enlightenment brings with it not only spiritual expansion, but also, at times, great shame.

All this awfulness is, of course, presented by Franco accompanied by alluring visuals and an appropriate music score. Beauty is wrought from ferocity.

Wherever Justine turns for help, she instead finds betrayal. The quest for kindness yields the fruit of victimization, from being robbed by a dissembling priest to being subjected to maniacal debauchery at the hands of a deranged monk played by Jack Palance.

The hapless Justine also ends up in the hands of Klaus Kinski, whose presence in this film is so natural and organic. He is an actor perfectly suited for such deranged cinema—or, rather, cinema about derangement (or what is only perceived as being deranged).

The story provides a relentless reminder of the evil that exists in the hearts of humanity. *Justine* is not a rejection of the existence of good, but a pointed reminder that we are each a yin-yang, of light and dark intermingled.

Justine's uber-innocence only answers half of the biblical injunction: to be as innocent as doves but as crafty as serpents. Regardless of one's "goodness" or lack of personal experience with devious ways, one should not be unfamiliar with the predatory, untrustworthy world that everyone inhabits, from the chaste virgin to the robber and rapist.

A curious cognitive dissonance in *Justine* is Franco's penchant for maintaining a relatively light and humorous mien, at least in some scenes. The lighter moments provide a startling juxtaposition that serves to heighten the impact of the abuse Justine suffers while also creating irony through the suggestion that there is a comic resonance between good and evil.

Justine is an impressive work. The film is an outstanding example, via its beauty and conceptual layers, of the type of textured and sublime filmmaking for which Franco had such a natural, innate gift.

This movie is not my favorite Franco piece, but I do submit that, in some ways, it represents the pinnacle of the director's expressive style, at least in regard to this particular mode of the filmmaker's cinematic creativity.

WOMEN IN CELLBLOCK 9 (1976)

As is obvious from the title, this movie is a Women-In-Prison (WIP) drama, one of several in Jess Franco's abundant canon.

Among the various subgenres of film that this amazing director prolifically produced and proffered to the rarified cult audience of the cinema strange and the art house cinema, was the WIP film.

Jess Franco's classic 99 *Women* was very much a seminal picture in that subversive WIP genre (but a subtextual one in Franco's capable hands). *Women of Cellblock 9* is a women in prison picture directed by the man who originally helped to shape and forge this subgenre. WIP is a category of film that remains influenced to this day (directly and indirectly) by this most singular filmmaker and creator of transcendent, hyperbolic, gonzo movie artistry.

Franco's work in this subgenre and the consequent influence of this work should lend some credibility to this movie—if you're unconvinced by my purple prose.

There are numerous WIP movies available for viewing: from the films that we refer to as the pioneering efforts in this subgenre (many of them excellent movies), to those that are derivative of these pioneering originals. Some of these derivative films are good and some are awful. Regardless of whether imitators were creatively inspired or financially inspired*, the number of WIP movies that appeared following the seminal efforts of films such as 99 *Women* have grown and reproduced rapidly.

Therefore we definitely have a subgenre loaded (if not a glutted) with numerous examples and variations on the basic theme. In addition to the relatively well-known (among genre-heads, anyway) examples of women-in-prison movies, there are also many obscure WIP movies, some them thematically overlapping as Nazisploitation movies. In any case, the WIP film and its variants hold a position of significant status

---

*Please note that I do not try to make an artistic distinction between those creatively inspired versus those inspired by the profit potential demonstrated by such a genre (i.e. "Hey, 99 *Women* made money, so let's make a movie like it and see if we can tap into the cash flow, too."). This happened in the slasher genre after *Halloween* was a success and *Friday the 13th* modeled itself on the former. Yet *Friday the 13th* was still an artistic endeavor without regard to money motive, as I discuss in depth in my book *Horror Is Art!*, also available from Book Devil Press.

in the underground movie culture.

Another WIP film by Franco is *Ilsa the Wicked Warden* (discussed in detail elsewhere in this book). This movie is an absolute classic of the genre, as well as being one Franco's more impactful and distinctive WIP efforts. *Ilsa the Wicked Warden* is noteworthy for being an unexpected combination of restraint and gut-wrenching horror.

Women in Cellblock 9 might, at least in some regards, be considered a more bare bones type of women-in-prison movie. But the film nevertheless demonstrates Franco's ability to make the most of the limited resources available to him and create a multi-faceted and textured work of full potency. Quite often in Franco's work it is the cinematography and visual structures that demonstrate his ability to use minimalist tools to create works of a truly robust nature.

Through the camera's eye, we observe scenes of torture in *Cellblock 9* that are, especially by Franco standards, comparatively "mild." But these sequences are still able, with a tight grip, to get a fist around your intestines and squeeze.

Franco tests us. It is part of his job as the outsider artist, to use one of his cinematic foci, to illuminate our darker and/or hidden natures. In this he takes special delight; it is a mission really, to expose us, with no hope of denial, to what dwells within each and every person watching his films.

There are even more graphic sequences in the film—such as the forcing a female inmate to lie on a bed with a large horn-shaped object at crotch-and-thigh level. But these sequences are less direct and visually horrifying than those that can be seen in any number of other films from this director. This scene, however, is made graphic and chilling though the generous presence of the blood on the table at crotch level. *Women of Cellblock 9* is not without its in-your-face moments.

I don't know which orifice–vagina or ass–is beleaguered in this torture scene. But I assume that vaginal penetration with what looks like a goddamned bull's horn would be pretty traumatic without adding anal violation to the process. The torturer and inventor of the nasty device being used, does say at one point, however, that every man he has used the device on has become a homosexual!

Subsequently, this cruel bastard abandons his invention's phallic use *à la* horn insertion, turning to something primitive and simple but equally appalling. With use of a tube he encourages a super-hungry rat to enter the inmate's vaginal canal and feast on a gourmet cervical smorgasbord.

Even with (again, by Franco standards) restraint, the movie is more than capable of grabbing you by the balls and clenching its cinematic fist.

THE CASTLE OF FU MANCHU (1969)

Here we have Jess Franco displaying his top technique for the multi-faceted application of skilled cinematography: drizzles of thick mood, the insertion of colorful characters and the creation of equally colorful scenarios in which to insert those characters.

This astounding filmmaker, with this film, returns to the pulp espionage genre. This is Franco's follow-up film to *The Blood of Fu Manchu*, a movie that featured none other than Christopher Lee. This is one of several times Franco made a casting coup and landed Lee to act in one of his pictures.

Appearing in the titular role as the dastardly and dangerous schemer Fu Manchu, the always marvelous Christopher Lee turns in a divinely exquisite performance as the famous vintage villain. His masterful portrayal oozes the rich and formidable screen presence that Lee always brought to his film portrayals. He was a master craftsman and watching him work is always a captivating experience.

Lee brings his full talents to this effort. Always a professional, he was not one to skimp on the use of his talent, be he playing Saruman in *Lord of the Rings* or in one of his roles in a Jess Franco picture.

The Castle of Fu Manchu finds the villainous Asian (the original literary character was a manifestation of the yellow peril fear evident in the pre-World War II era) up to his kimono sleeves in another far-reaching, high-tech, James Bond-type-villain scheme to effect a controlled chaos that will lead to his world domination.

Fu Manchu certainly sets his sights high.

With a deadly powerful new technology right at his fingertips—a technology upon which he of course holds a monopoly—Fu Manchu is prepared to dole out some mass destruction the moment he feels froggy enough. This ambitious arch villain sets about blackmailing and holding the entire damn globe hostage to his evil.

This pay-up-or-else bad guy has a nasty weapon he would be more than happy to demonstrate on a large scale, which would make a lot of people dead, or at least pretty unhappy.

James Bond really should have had a chance to go head-to-head with Fu Manchu. It would have been quite the match made in hell and heavenly viewing. What pulp espionage fan would want to miss such a showdown as that?

Events kick off with a truly exciting and eye-grabbing attack on a large ship, which sinks under the pressure of Fu Manchu's ferocity-laden attack. But his ferocity is, of course, controlled. Fu Manchu is a precise, intelligent villain and driven by megalomaniacal goals.

Sadly, author and Fu Manchu-creator Sax Rohmer was not alive to see the day when Franco would bring his classic villain of literature to life on the screen in that special Franco fashion.

Franco was not the first filmmaker to adapt Fu Manchu to the big screen, but not having seen non-Franco film interpretations of the super villain, I can damn well guarantee you that Franco's vision of Fu Manchu is unique and distinctive among its cinematic peers.

At any rate, I would love to know what Sax Rohmer would have thought about Franco's silver screen take on Fu Manchu.

NIGHT HAS A THOUSAND DESIRES (1984)

This plot proves to be an ideal method for merging Franco's aptitude for burying plots within thick strands of erotic and violent surrealism. He suggests a topic, then than rather than simply telling you a tale, he unleashes an intense experiential expression of the story.

It is almost as though he was trying to recreate the experience of collective memory through psychedelic cinema.

Franco creates rushes of images and sound that transcend any mere story plot. These are experiential works of art.

Night Has a Thousand Desires has a plot that readily lends itself to this technique. We observe the female lead Irina (Lina Romay) as a women plagued by dream visions that begin as sensual erotic encounters, intense and electric, but end in climatic acts of violence.

Whether we are watching a gorgeously filmed orgy or an intimate coupling of fellatio (just off screen, but suggested with real erotic classiness), these scenes of lush sexual encounter culminate in violence.

There is in this film a particularly dreamy dovetailing of the threads of Eros and Thanatos that Franco ties together with a passionate devotion to his craft and his vision. His artistic endeavor on film is, of course, a manifestation of the singular and indescribable vision possessed by this cinematic luminary, and by which he is possessed.

The cinematography utilized here and the darkly psychedelic oddball score (which helps weaves the dream sensation), combine to create a spooky, but absorbing and darkly titillating, work of art. There are music and images in this film that the moviegoer is not apt to forget, at least not in the foreseeable future.

And as for the ethereal, hypnotic story, the viewer is lulled into a place where you are not only drowning in eddies of liquid mood, but you are learning to breathe cinema as if through gills. The viewer is also psychically aroused and anxiously curious to discover how the leading lady's visions of sex culminating in murder will next manifest themselves.

And purely in regard to the film's conjuring of cinematic erotic atmosphere, *Night Has a Thousand Desires* proves incredibly supercharged with scenes that will transport you to a far point in the cosmos while also touching you intimately.

The viewer finds himself in a place of keen awareness where you are not only artistically and spiritually elevated, but where you are aglow with potent erotic energy. This film arguably features some of Franco's

NIGHT HAS A THOUSAND DESIRES

Lina Romay in *The Night Has a Thousand Desires*.

finest tenebrous eroticism.

This is an extremely immersive movie, with sequences of such enthrallment that they light up and create a direct connection between your uppermost lotus chakra and your heated core of erotic electricity.

The film is inspiring art with the sexual power of quality pornography.

But make no mistake, *Night Has a Thousand Desires* is *not* porn.

However, the film is capable of viscerally attacking your libido with all the blaze of porn prurience, but it does so as part of a more expansive experience that emblazons the carnal-spiritual yin-yang inside your chest, through your eyes and groin and through your body and soul.

This movie is a sterling example of Jess Franco's penetrating talent.

FACELESS (1987)

With *Faceless* we see Franco delivering one of his rarer genre projects, as this movie resembles an American-influenced horror film along the lines of a gory semi-slasher.

This film even has Telly Savalas!

The plot—and this is one of Franco's linear films—involves a mad doctor ensconced in his evil clinic where he conducts skin graft surgery on the women he has kidnapped. It goes without saying that the surgery always ends badly for the women.

Mutilation abounds.

This is among Franco's more fun films, and it is always enjoyable to watch the versatile director tip his hat to the American world of horror cinema.

Not surprisingly, Franco also includes a police procedural subplot, a story component that the director frequently includes in his horror endeavors. Some of these sequences lean more toward having a *giallo* flavor. Of course, the spaghetti thriller genre was a partial prototype (add some Hitchcock, etc.) for the America slasher genre.

Therefore the integration of distinctly U.S.-flavored horror thrills with the classic *giallo* mien is an organic intertwining of styles. This proves to be a winning combination in Jess Franco's capable hands.

Despite *Faceless* not being a conventional Franco movie, he still works in some of his recurring themes. The mad-scientist-skin-graft plot recalls some of the early gothic films directed by the filmmaker.

And the familiar situation of violent, transgressive medical experimentation pops up not only here and in his gothic films (and in his monster movie homages), but in other genres, such as the women-in-prison category, including his *Ilsa the Wicked Warden*, a movie that features some very disturbing scenes.

The surgery plot allows for some ghastly—and quite gory—operation sequences. We witness a surgical failure scene in which a still living woman's skin falls to pieces in an attempt to remove it from her face; this is a dreadfully grisly bit.

Also grim is the wrap-up of a sequence in which the mad doctor's big, dumb brute helper performs the dismemberment and disposal of a body. He must be a lonely bastard, given that he feels compelled to give the decapitated head, with its mangled visage, a wee smooch on the face.

Yick.

Of course, given the nature of this genre's obligatory inclusion of big, dumb brute characters, I could have probably predicted a zero love life for the fellow even before seeing him woo a chopped-off head.

Needless to say, this is one of Franco's carnage-filled flicks. His horror violence is often disturbing without being uber-gory. This one, though, is like *Bloody Moon*, in that they both have American-style slasher leanings and both explore graphic violence.

Franco succeeds with flying colors in both cases.

And since *Faceless* is not "just" a gore film and since it is enriched with Francoan film flavor, it is superior to so many of the gore vehicles that glut the extreme horror market.

The denouement is an exercise in pure psychological terror. The director faces no challenge in blending horrifying physical violence with gut-chilling psycho-horror.

The conclusion is coldly dark, black as starless night and as cold as the absolute zero of deepest space.

Faceless is like something out of Poe. More than one something out of Poe. The worse part is that the victim of this last devilment didn't even get a consolation bottle of amontillado.

This one belongs on the list of my favorite Jess Franco films.

EUGÉNIE DE SADE (1973)

Eugénie de Sade is, obviously, another of Franco's Marquis de Sade-based movies, of which, as you surely know at this point, there were quite a few.
This movie features one of the filmmaker's preferred themes: transgression. The core characters are a stepfather and stepdaughter who have a rather unhealthy relationship. She quite willingly plucks the innocence from the core of her own soul when she explores her father's library of libertine literature.
During her process of self-discovery, she discovers that her stepfather's interest in the ever-heady combination of sex-and-death is more than merely academic. He is into it full tilt.
Dad is primed for full-on murderous erotic binges. Dad is also sociopathic when pursuing his S&M tastes. This is a match made in hell. Dad and daughter soon emerge as a team of sexually charged killers.
This is the fertile soil to which Franco returns again and again. His masterpieces of de Sadean cinema are bold, subversive-thinking journeys into other dimensions where Thanatos and dark Eros embrace and meld with each other to create ouroboros swirls of energy that reflect our inner, lower and upper cores of sensual and spiritual energy.
Franco, once again, is bold and evolutionary and revolutionary.
And no matter how many times Franco returns to till the rich earth of the shadow Eros, it remains fertile in his loving and far-seeing hands.
The world needs Jess Franco. Specifically the world of art, but also the world at large.
The world is a better place with Franco in it.
And as might be expected, there is a nightclub scene. But I bet you already knew that.
It is a given that Franco applies his always spectacular audio-visual genius to the exploration of psychosexuality. *Eugénie de Sade* is resplendent in its visual glory, bold in its lush color and composition. This film is an allure to the senses with its scoring always perfectly matched with the visuals. Franco stuns with his cinematic eye and also, *of course*, strikes us dead center with an erotic energy supercharged by its synergistic relationship with subversive contexts.
The film is headier than dwarven mead.
There is a sequence in which dad and daughter hire a model (actually a hooker) and you can bet she is in for more than she bargained for in

this deal with the devil. Or devils. The stepdad commences to take pictures of the model in poses suggesting violent sadism, while his daughter looks on approvingly, a cold, deep look in her eyes.

Jess Franco's filming of a photographer capturing such images creates a metatextual layer. Here we behold this purveyor of challenging and disturbing erotica looking through his camera at a character looking through *his* camera at the creation of his own dark erotic art.

Eugénie de Sade is also rife with Franco's penchant for juxtaposing upbeat frolicking scenes with more trippy, tenebrous sequences as the film reaches deep into its shadowy cave and casts light upon the grimmer side of sexuality.

BARBED WIRE DOLLS (1976)

Franco frequently returned to his work in the women-in-prison genre. He not only helped kick-start the whole genre in its modern incarnation, but he continued to work in the genre, maintaining his ongoing influence over WIP development.

The director has thoroughly explored the theme of unjust imprisonment and unjust imprisonment is one of the most psychologically terrifying concepts I can imagine. The idea of being imprisoned unfairly and then being tortured—the terror not only physical but also psychological—and in addition, not having any recourse for appeal is an appalling fate to experience or even contemplate experiencing.

The tortures inflicted here include taunting the prisoners with food, creating terrible humiliating personal situations, forced lesbianism, and so much more. *Barbed Wire Dolls* is a sucker punch of depravity.

Franco's film, while not depraved itself, is an exercise in exploring one of the director's beloved themes. Again, as with many other Franco movies, he is unabashedly ripping the veil from the shadow side of the human soul.

The tortures are brutal and shocking at times, and unpredictable. Franco finds creative ways to depict torture and humiliation and uses them as a stabbing device to penetrate our psychological innards with his horrors of the human soul exposed.

The cruelty and violence of which we are capable might not be unlimited—but who knows? Mankind's potential for cruelty and violence has certainly proved expansive. The human spirit is capable of great good ... and, unfortunately, terrible evil.

A gritty, frank and unashamed movie like this is the kind of cinematic artwork that directly punches through to the center of our nature, harshly and without apology, to show us some uncomfortable truths about ourselves. To the uninitiated, however, the film may seem like pure sleaze.

But *Barbed Wire Dolls* is more than sleaze. A topic as deliberately ugly and provocative as this one is perfect for striking a chord of repulsion and recoil in a very direct manner. Franco's skillful touch empowers the material and makes what is vile into something that is, paradoxically, art and beauty.

If truth is beauty, then there is some very ugly beauty out there, inside and outside of art.

BARBED WIRE DOLLS

The parade of cruel scenes is a parade of human atrocity and the potential thereof is writ large across the screen in symbolic, mythic form. If every movie was puppy dogs and big red hearts (the Valentine's Day sort, not the ripped-out variety) then our personal subconscious and our collective subconscious are both denied a vital, productive and creative outlet.

Art is created to cheer us up and entertain us, but it can also be created to illuminate. Often the resulting illumination is contrary to cheerful expression. Sometimes illumination requires that which is cold, ruthless and uncomfortable.

HOW TO SEDUCE A VIRGIN (1973)

If the movie has a torture dungeon and the movie is directed by Jess Franco, you know you can be pretty sure that you are about to enjoy a quality picture.

If the movie stars a crazy sadist bitch who loves the S&M subculture—sub-subculture since she doesn't give a damn if her submissives are willing masochists or not—and if the film is directed by Jess Franco, that you can expect good stuff.

The title of this film is a wonderful piece of irony, smirking in its understatedness and with a fire in its loins over the vast and vicious grimness lying in the subtext. The title is virtually a "polite" riff on the arc of this movie.

A psychopath with a hunger for non-consenting sadism plies her trade on the innocent nymphet daughter of some friends.

A virgin to target for "seduction."

As might be expected, Franco is right at home here in this vivid tale of innocence dashed and enlightenment earned amidst a river of blood and tears.

I also doubt you suffered a heart attack when you encountered the moody score, the director's sharp eye for that which is being filmed, the daring and delicate threads of consciousness-spreading witch's brew, the bold strokes of loving defiance in the face of the moral conventions that daily squeeze our throats, and the overall air of an otherworldly something permeating the film.

How to Seduce a Virgin contains some images that are among the most striking in Franco's filmography. The score is varied but always hits a bull's eye by enhancing the other elements of the film in conjuring the appropriate atmosphere.

This film, like oh-so-many of Jess Franco's brilliant art house supernovas, lies effectively beyond words when attempting to appropriately describe the experience—he says while trying to use words to describe his experience.

Franco's best work, and indeed the bulk of his films, is transcendent in one manner or another. *How to Seduce a Virgin* is absolutely no exception. And while it has connections with so many layers of Franco's perennial themes, it still boasts its own lucid personality in the great sea of outsider cinema.

The filmmaker's work almost seems to be a great ocean above and around us with swirls of water coiling in on themselves, the whole

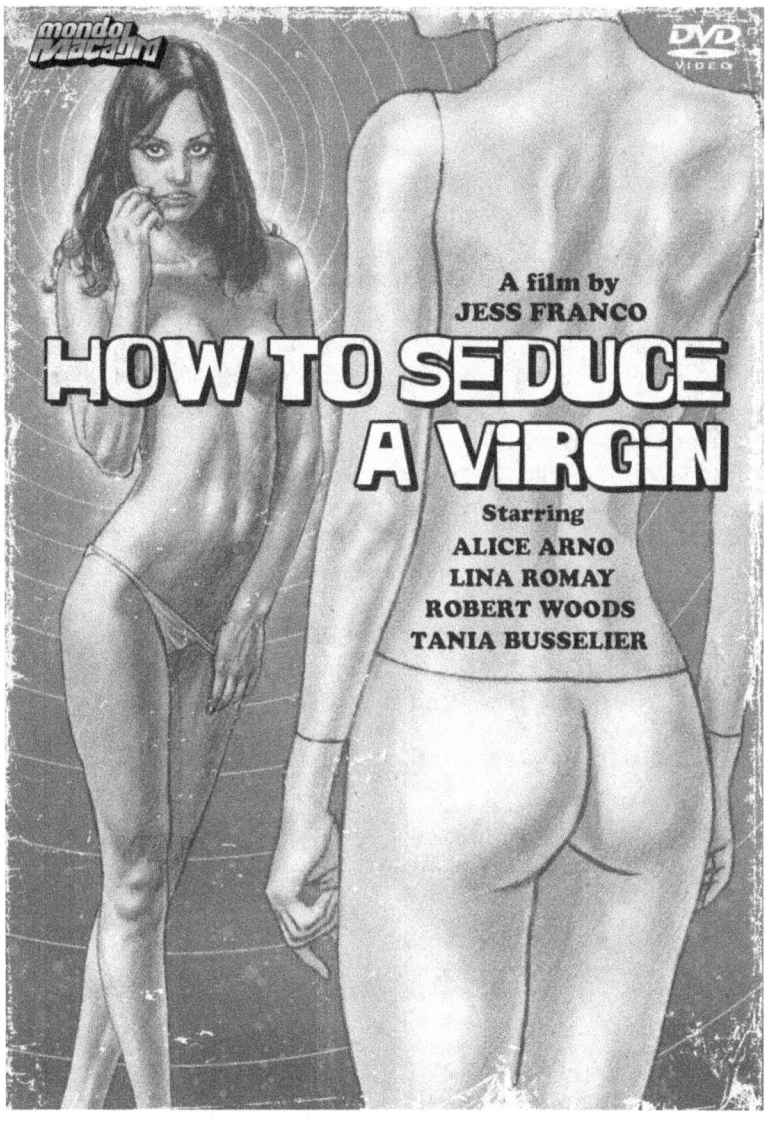

DVD art for Mondo Macabro's release of *How to Seduce a Virgin*.

experience like a tide turning in on itself, a great psychedelic oroborous constantly recreating itself, embodying something greater than all the individual pieces of the whole ….

   There is nothing like a Franco film—I am pretty sure this is not the first time I've said that—and not infrequently a Franco film is nothing like other Franco films, even while being innately similar. They are related in the DNA of film and onscreen narrative, distinguished by the powerful auteur's vision that permeates this collective which has arisen from the combined force of the director's cumulative works.

He makes me wax eloquent.

He makes violence sexuality eloquent.

He makes the shadows, outside and inward, eloquent.

Franco's work is cinematic poetry and of such sway and influence that the words of a mere film essayist strain to flow from their prose tracks into the winged hyperbole of the poetic.

No adjective alone is adequate. No linear string of descriptive words may do more than: (a) at best, sling a month's worth of words-of-the-day at like-minded language junkies, or (b) at worst, spin out a slab of self-indulgent prose that leaves the reader no more enlightened at the end than at beginning.

And so all those adjectives and expressions strain to be free of the embarrassing confines of the essayist's prose and yearn to eddy together in a leaf-on-the-breeze dance that strikes visual flares—ascendant imagery that speaks volumes more than the literal tendencies of mere words ever could.

Now then, in fear of having trod down that path of unforgiveable self-indulgence (for I know I have already dipped my toe in those waters, but I sincerely hope that I am not drowning you in that ocean), I will ...

Shut myself down ... or continue to spew purple verbiage at you and hope you are as ecstatic as I ...

... as ecstatic as a Jess Franco film.

As ecstasy consumed ... as in *How to Seduce a Virgin*.

THE SINISTER EYES OF DR. ORLOFF (1973)

A wall of atmosphere gets all up in your face with the brusque but spartan opening title sequence of Franco's 1973 entry in his Dr. Orloff franchise. The series has featured some strong work from the filmmaker and his *The Awful Dr. Orloff* is a seminal work of horror—a tipping point not only Jess Franco, but also for Spanish horror.

Jess Franco just might be *the* best thing to ever happen to Spanish horror cinema.

The film certainly represented a vanguard effort toward a fresh, new, sharp and darker neo-gothic horror. *The Sinister Eyes of Dr. Orloff* launched Franco internationally.

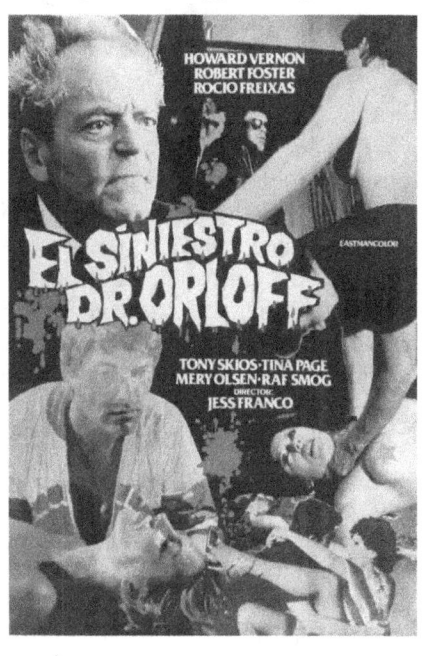

So with this film, we find the man faithfully paying tribute to a character and series to which he owes much.

Dr. Orloff is up to his armpits in his usual ... er ... typical ...

Dr. Orloff is up to his armpits in the kinds of gonzo science gone out of its mind and totally off the rails, wacko science that has gotten him—and everybody around him—in deep trouble during each of these outings.

(Hell, Orloff wasn't even in *The Diabolical Dr. Z*, except that it is Orloff's science on which Dr. Z's work is based. But Orloff's presence and influence are dominant: we sense a disturbance through its dark power. Except that dark equals cool in this case.)

Quite gothic oppression keeps its arid but pervasive mood on hand throughout the film as this modern 20th Century gothic reveals its creepy tale of terror.

One of the horror components featured in *The Sinister Eyes of Dr. Orloff* is that of using mesmerism to spread whatever diabolical mayhem the doc has up his lab coat sleeves for this outing on the silver screen. Poking around inside of people's heads is—surprise, surprise, he says with a straight face,—the kind of chaos-producing behavior that will lead to violent and deadly results.

As stated above—but why not reinforce it?—life just does not end nicely for much of anybody in the vicinity of one of Mad Doc Orloff's lunatic schemes.

With Franco in charge, we are treated to another example of neo-classic evil scientist cinema that the filmmaker has created on several occasions when honoring—as he never got tired of doing—the monster-and-mad-doctor classics from both the U.S. and Britain, classics that had a very real impact on several aspects of his filmmaking.

The Sinister Eyes of Dr. Orloff features a notable music score—a strangely atmospheric score that exists in synergy with other aspects of the film. This is NOT an alien concept for Jess Franco, as we know.

But while not surprising us with his skillful melding of mood and music, he does surprise us with the very startling direction he takes by using the type of music he implements in this cinematic story. There is a sense of cognitive dissonance when one hears *folk music* accompanying the events that unfold during the movie.

At first, hearing folk music in a Jess Franco film is truly and sharply startling, but you quickly sink in, settle in and wrap yourself up warmly with the peculiar way this music works with and enhances the total film experience.

The Sinister Eyes of Dr. Orloff is one of Franco's quiet pieces.

If this is gonzo film-making—and it is—it is nevertheless done with some subtlety. Because the film maintains a restrained but tense energy level while relating its story, it is deceptive how gonzo the movie actually is.

By virtue of its reserved nature, *The Sinister Eyes of Dr. Orloff* earns itself some distinction in the world of Jess Franco.

LORNA THE EXORCIST (1974)

Lorna the Exorcist is Franco's take on the classic Faustian tale of making a deal with the devil regretting it. This is a theme one could hardly expect the likes of Jess Franco to ignore.

The deal diabolicalus that lies at the center of *Lorna*'s psycho-visceral supernatural horror story is this: nineteen years ago a man made a deal with a devil named Lorna and that deal garnered him riches at a casino. He now returns to the same locale with his 18-year-old daughter.

I guess you know damned well what he promised for his wealth, don't you?

Rather than the classic trope of selling one's soul—a very viable archetype—the misguided dealmaker daddy offered his then as-yet-unborn child. This concept alone is chilling and here it is given the full Franco treatment.

An atmosphere of dread conveyed by the filmmaker's tried and true techniques bolsters the already doom-laden story. A claustrophobic feeling is created that dominates the key scenes doused in perilous mood.

Lorna the Exorcist is a haunting film and it haunts in the way only a Franco-fest can. He creates a stark, experiential reality of ominous portent and hopeless inevitability.

That the promised daughter is having confusing psychic experiences in which she is connected to Lorna the devil makes the proceedings even creepier. Here is a girl who has no idea why her dad has dragged her off to this mysterious appointment and who certainly has no knowledge that she has been sacrificed, if not literally on an altar, then effectively by dint of her doom as a servant to evil.

This is one huge alarming scenario.

NIGHTMARES COME AT NIGHT (1972)

Nightmares Come at Night seems predictive of *Night Has a Thousand Desires*, which was made twelve years later. Both films feature a woman entrapped by bizarre dreams of ultra-sexuality that are connected with acts of violence. Reality and fantasy play slip-slide as the woman is overwhelmed by her dreadful visions.

Intense mood is evident from the beginning and we are plunged into a sea of grim erotica and its Thanatos complement. *Nightmares Come at Night* is a spicy drink from which to cinematically sip, and the concoction goes down strong but sweet.

The movie is possessed of gripping imagery throughout. It also has—and don't ask me to elucidate because I wouldn't know how—a distinctive flavor among Franco's films. The film is distinct, not as superior to the rest, but simply in the sense that it does not get lost in

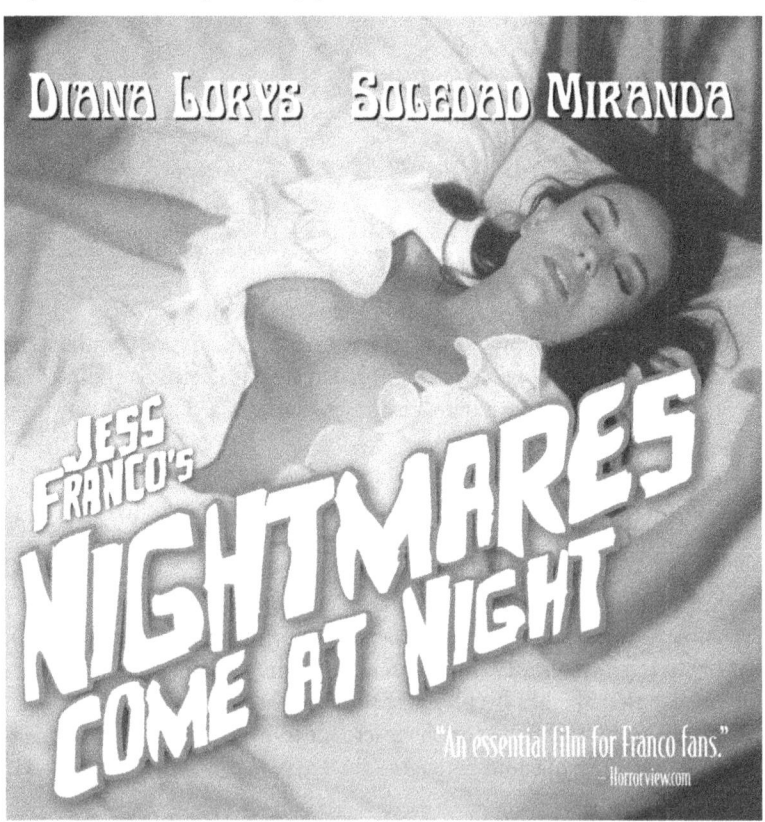

the shuffle of the vast expanse of his work. The film has a very memorable tone, to say the least.

Yes, of course, it is utterly Franco all the way.

Light and color and shadow in simple but elegant compositions within the camera's eye, and on your television screen, create images to quench your ocular thirst. Franco, as you might predict, shows us some beautiful and hard-to-forget images.

The central character is—shocker—a nightclub performer. And this avant-garde theater features a trippy erotic act by a woman who is drowning in scary visions, at the end of her rope and doing a job she has come to hate.

The nightclub act is one of the more striking take away images from the film.

All of this imagery finds itself spinning around a mysterious hub—a strange woman who inserts herself into the beleaguered heroine's life. Things become progressively more peculiar as the Eros and Thanatos quotient rises dramatically.

Nightmares Come at Night is an exercise in introspective mood, psychosexual fear, shadow exploration and the earthy but paralyzing terror of losing one's mind.

Franco's natural talent for crafting erotic art is on full display here. There are some riveting tableaus crackling with erotic energy, like lightning bolts from belly to TV, TV to belly. The film sends smooth, sensual shocks of erotic potency through the ether, enveloping your mind and lighting up your nervous system.

Nightmares Come at Night is not one of Jess Franco's best-known films, but it deserves to be seen. It is alive with the kind of vibe that the filmmaker was always able to summon seemingly from thin air, right out of the bubbling quantum foam.

Amidst all this headiness there is also an ordinary (relatively speaking) subplot of a criminal with a greed-fueled nature. This subplot provides a stark contrast to the prevailing dark etherea.

The movie is a quietly ecstatic mystery—a mystery of both crime and mind.

REVENGE IN THE HOUSE OF USHER (1983)

Jess Franco's twist on Edgar Allan Poe is also the spiritual successor to the director's Dr. Orloff franchise.

The core element from Poe's story is present and accounted for: an old mind, deranged and senile, slips into unreality. Around the failing man with the failing mind is the decaying manse that serves as the outward symbol of his fracturing psychology and his tenuous grip on reality.

The shadows of the gloomy castle are those of batshit old Usher's degenerating, guilt-stricken brain as it veers helplessly toward sheer insanity.

Echoes of *Dracula* are also to be discovered in *Revenge in the House of Usher*. But these echoes are not in the strictly classic vampiric sense, as you might expect.

Instead the parallel with *Dracula* lies in the guise of a young man visiting a strange castle with a strange host (Howard Vernon as Eric Usher) and thus exposing himself to unexpected horror. And we are delighted once again to have Lina Romay on hand as Maria the housekeeper to shed some light, via her beauty, on the gloomy goings-on.

The curiously named visitor—Alan *Harker*—may not be confronting fangs and blood-drinking but there is another kind of blood-thief entirely, and a motive that has nothing to do with thirst. This is another imaginative reconstruction from the ever-creative Jess Franco.

Vampirism is sublimated and breaks a cocoon as an entirely different entity, something new and different. For Franco this is a marvelously dovetailed reimagining of both his mad scientist film concepts and the classic Stoker novel.

Franco bucks cinematic narrative here with a method he used from time to time, but in this film there is a stout example on hand. The director was known to recycle leftover footage from one movie for another one.

Old black-and-white *Orloff* footage is re-contexted in *Revenge in the House of Usher*. In this film, the recycled footage appears as a series of flashback sequences rearranged as a subplot to further this uniquely Francoan interpretation of Poe.

Franco also revisits the classic horror motif of killing women in an effort to help a beloved daughter or wife be freed of an ailment. This time it isn't skin-grafts or such, but rather stolen blood—which of course results in death for the female "donors."

Usher is applying the skills he got with his mad scientist diploma to seek a method, however ghastly, to bring the daughter he adores out of her coma.

Meanwhile, his wife *still* nags at him from the grave and he must also contend with the angry spirits of the women he has destroyed in his wretched quest to save his daughter at their expense.

This is a stylish, atmospheric gothic from a filmmaker who has time and again demonstrated his talent for putting the gothic on film in ways all his own.

The cinematography, as usual, is above par and a siren song for the eyes. This is a visually sumptuous film, but rejects any need for ostentation.

Dense mood permeates all.
Creepy music aids and abets.
Dank castle walls bring the chill.
Check. Check. And check.

All in all there is some mighty fine work done by this filmmaker in *Revenge in the House of Usher*. You can fall in love with Franco all over again just with some of the images and scenes he sprinkles generously throughout the movie.

THE SADISTIC BARON VON KLAUS (1962)

This film is early vintage Franco.

The Sadistic Baron Von Klaus is considered to be the first Spanish horror film. But even considering that this film was produced in an earlier era and given its relatively mild nature (by Franco standards), it is still a shocker. Certainly this is an edgy film, especially by the American standards of the time.

I have a hard time believing that this film would have gotten much play in the U.S. in 1962, although the country was on the verge of a movie-making breakthrough in what would become known as the "exploitation" film era.

The degree of sadism shown in the last reel (even if mild by modern parameters) is pretty startling. To see flogging and nudity combined in an old black-and-white picture *is* rather shocking.

The opening credits unfold with a stationary shot of a man playing the piano. The scene is somewhat somber and most definitely a brooding, moody piece. A tone has certainly been set for the story that is about to play out before the viewer, even if one has no idea what that story might be.

The piano sequence concludes with the man pulling his hands very slowly away from the keys after finishing the piece of music that he has been playing throughout this opening shot.

It is as if he is possessed of some unknown dread, some fear or trepidation that was stilled or suppressed while his hands could dance over the keys, but which has now become manifest at the cessation of his playing—as though the music has soothed whatever disturbance has sent these trembles of anxiety through him.

Or else the music is itself a compulsion which always drains strength from the piano player.

The symbolism can be sorted out however you wish in the greater context of the film's story, but however you understand this low-key but compelling opening imagery, the aspect of abiding fear is apparent throughout the piano player's daily life. The obvious heavy weight of suffering or anxiety that exists alongside the casual playing of the piano forms is very moving group of images.

This is a powerful, wordless opening scene, of minimalist production, but filled with metacontent and emotional energy. Without relaying a single bit of fact or information, *The Sadistic Baron Von Klaus* has already established an atmosphere of anxiety, setting the viewer on

edge—a viewer who doesn't even know yet why he or she *should be* fearful for with the piano player (identity yet unknown).

The plot about to reveal itself over the course of the movie involves a string of awful murders that have shaken up the village of Holfen.

For the local people, these deaths inspire superstitious fears that the area might still be haunted by the curse of a baron who dwelt there in the 1600s. He was a notorious villain who kept a torture dungeon for indulging his darkest desires. This sadistic baron has inspired many legends, tales of sacrifice and supernatural doings. The memory of this man, at the very least, remains embedded in the hearts and minds of the people, whether or not there is an actual supernatural presence to be reckoned with.

The murders have a different effect on a policeman who is doggedly determined to get to solve them, and who thinks that the solution lies not with the lingering evil presence of a dead man, but rather with the evil that lives in the heart of a living man. This particular man is, of course, a descendent of the wicked Baron Von Klaus. The officer is afraid, perhaps even convinced, that the baron's descendent may have taken up his ancestor's peccadilloes.

A touching scene occurs in the film when the present Von Klaus is warned by a dying relative that his family has a nasty past and that he should flee from this legacy—get out now, before the same tendencies overtake and overpower him.

The relative, an old woman near death, wishes to convince young Von Klaus that the horrible essence pulsing through his genes may be a haunting supernatural presence or may simply be a family-historical curse that will eventually drive the man headlong into the old Von Klaus lifestyle.

She offers a long-kept secret—a key.

The key that will open the cellar.

Her intent is to provide a warning regarding the secrets of the torture basement and this revelation is intended to be cautionary—but one can't help but wonder if the exploration of the long-hidden cellar by the young Von Klaus will lead to his doom.

The theme of inherited evil plaguing a family, however its transmission, is an old theme for humankind. In today's world, we know about genes and how certain less than savory proclivities, along with more positive traits, can be passed on to the unwary.

We also know from long, hard experience that certain behaviors can be passed on, not genetically, but through direct experience. An abusive parent can forge an abusive child, a vicious cycle begging to be broken.

Can a legacy also be passed on simply through the knowledge of a rotten apple or two in one's family? Can a familial reputation cause evil to be passed on simply because it haunts the collective memory of the family?

Do the sins of the father infect the children for generations afterward?

These are the types of intriguing questions Franco is pondering in *The Sadistic Baron Von Klaus*. This film also provides a vehicle for him to explore the themes that would stay with him throughout his career. Even in 1962, the filmmaker is playing with the ideas of dark human desire and sado-masochism. He is also doing so in a gothic context, presenting another of his recurring film styles. It is arguably his early canon that is most saturated with gothic cinema, although his mid-career monster movies also perpetuate his love for gothic cinema and storytelling.

And, as noted in other early Franco endeavors, his sense of visual style is mixed with the right complement of musical accompaniment and is already well-developed right from the beginning of his career. Although Franco later distinguished himself using lush color cinematography, he was also supremely skilled in the manipulation of black-and-white cinematography. His use of light and shadow creates stunning vistas from apparently mundane objects and backgrounds. But whether filming a bad baron's dungeon or a lady's boudoir, the visual effect is always striking.

The director is already a master of mood this early in his career. The low-key but steady generation of the subtle sense of building doom is impeccably crafted. Suspense mounts deliberately but effectively, drawing the viewer into a place where you are both enthralled by cinematic beauty and captive to a growing, shadowy fear.

Creation of mood is a topic much harped upon here, certainly, but I cannot discuss *The Sadistic Baron Von Klaus*—along with *The Awful Dr. Orloff*, *The Diabolical Dr. Z*, and others—without illustrating how Jess Franco vividly demonstrates the depth and range of his talent as a filmmaker. He can engross you quietly with a detuned gothic thriller or mesmerize you into psychedelic godhood with a surrealist sex-and-death scene.

The breadth of the man's talent never ceases to impress. He is able to brilliantly realize ideas that in many other filmmakers' hands would fall flat or fail miserably. In a way, Franco is an absurdist. Even plot-centric and relatively un-crazy movies like *Dr. Z* will have gonzo components. Franco was, in part, channeling the campy sci-fi films from 1950s America, even while injecting the subtle flavors of gothic nuance into his films.

Flexible and versatile, Jess Franco cannot be denied his place among the great and unique filmmakers of the world.

Even at the level of basic mystery, *The Sadistic Baron Von Klaus* functions beautifully. The film is a real smooth operation to say the least. Franco knows how create cinematic flow and fluid narrative, whether surreal or rooted in story and plot.

There remains, as the story is still opening and revealing its secrets, a question as to whether what seems obvious is really the case. The modern mind wants to reject supernatural explanations—even more so, perhaps, when framed in a non-supernatural police procedural/noir context—and the modern mind certainly does not wish to be aligned or associated with the superstitious "common" mind.

And so, you will not be surprised to find yourself wanting to side with the investigator. As one of the two core characters around which the film revolves, he seems to represent the voice of reason. This is the siren song that lulls us into agreeing with him: it *must* be the modern Von Klaus picking up the thread left lying by the long-dead sadistic ancestor.

Yet we also can find sympathy for the Von Klaus descendent, who appears to be a sincere, moral figure—and one who anguishes over the hovering threat of the Von Klaus "curse." There is a very real chance, we feel, that he is innocent.

Franco develops a profound sense of suspense which provides a strong hook at the center of the tale, cloaked in a shroud of mystery and atmosphere. Franco may often dazzle and confound with elliptical surrealism without concrete resolution, but this film alone is able to verify that Franco was also completely capable of drawing you in with a good, old-fashioned story, using its secrets to titillate until the time arrives for their unveiling.

Equally effective are the frighteningly quiet scenes of victims being stalked in the still of the night while the town sleeps. The lack of a musical score or any other sound beyond the click of heels on a sidewalk or the flick of a light switch, creates a great space to be filled by atmosphere and chilling suspense. The stark tension grows, stretching the viewer tight as taut wire, awaiting the burst that will snap it in twain.

With Franco at the helm, this film is also edgier than its contemporaries. Nudity in sadistic contexts—Franco inserts the Eros-Thanatos dichotomy into his early career films —occurs, timed so as to surprise you once you have become acclimatized to the overall reserved mien of the film. These sequences are not as graphic as those that would come later in his career, but they are still psychologically disturbing and have a potent shock value, especially considering that this was 1962.

The Sadistic Baron Von Klaus is, without a doubt, one of Franco's best. The film also deserves to be ranked with other classic crime and gothic horror films—from any period.

THE HOT NIGHTS OF LINDA (1975)

The Hot Nights of Linda, is one of Franco's softer explorations of psychosexual deviance, at least tonally.

We have in this movie a wonderful Franco-wrought combination of characters: a beautiful young woman just looking for a secretarial job (i.e. she is just a "normal" person—one who has yet to cross the threshold of transgression). We also have a rich old man, her employer, whose soul is on fire with the torments of his inner demons, the wealthy man's two daughters—one a nymphomaniac and the other an invalid and finally, a speechless manservant who just grunts to indicate his intentions.

The grunting servant character is not unique to this Franco film. Nor

Lina Romay in *The Hot Nights of Linda*.

are some of its other elements. This one is just a bit less "in-your-face" than some of the director's other excursions into this sort of material.

Of course, once the new girl is settled into her new digs at the millionaire's home—actually, she is barely settled in before it is obvious that this family has its own strange dynamics—she is subjected to the bizarre influences of this dysfunctional family.

The dysfunctional family is another topic one finds Franco exploring in many of his films.

Hot Nights is arguably less vicious than some of the filmmaker's other examinations of perversion, but we do witness more than lesbian acts or a vampire on a bloody romp. And the violent Thanatos side of this movie's tale is not limited to the women.

A striking flogging scene in this picture depicts the whipping of the manservant, who has incurred the wrath of the family he serves. Jess Franco may adore his women and the fiendish sexual situations in which he places them, but his characters can still be equal opportunity torturers.

In some ways the whipping of a naked man is even more disturbing than watching bloody lashes appear across the skin of a beautiful female body, at least for me.

The sadistic nature of the scene of a naked man being flagellated conjures its own unarousing sexual mien, which can add an extra layer to the visceral, reptile-brain discomfort for hetero men. For gay men, the dynamic may well be reversed, though I wouldn't hazard to say one way or another.

I am not in a position to say with certainty.

Behind the unconventional sexual dynamics lies the family secret of murder. These people are not only sexual outliers, but they also seem to have a closer relationship to death than most people.

A question manifests itself in the movie: Who killed the millionaire's wife?

Haunting dreams of sex touched by death and/or violence (an associate of death)—one of Franco's most beloved themes—also materialize in *The Hot Nights of Linda*.

Sexual innocence being assailed by powerful counter-normal eroticism is also one of Franco's oft-revisited themes, and in this film we view a dreamy excursion beyond the bounds of mainstream Eros. The director topples all traditional familial boundaries even while deconstructing broader sexual values.

Not only are cultural sex norms being challenged, but also the very intimate nature of relationships between family members.

Franco also destroys personal barriers with his themes of innocence undone by strangers or new people in a character's life—i.e. an intimate part of a person's soul is forever altered by someone who is/was not an intimate, but who nevertheless becomes one by a direct invasion of the initiate's center, bypassing all emotional gateways.

The director, it appears, is using the erosion of family barriers as a microcosmic example of the ripping asunder of social parameters on a larger scale. Franco is jousting with unnecessarily conservative values and examples of cultural moral hypocrisy.

Just as the thieves of innocence invade the intimacies of their young subjects in his movies, Franco penetrates our own core by targeting one of the most intimate units in society's structure—the family.

COUNTESS PERVERSE (1974)

Countess Perverse is a much earlier adaptation by Franco of 1932's *The Most Dangerous Game* than is his film *Tender Flesh* (1997), also discussed in this book. The director applies his cinematic skills with sparse yet stunning fashion to this classic tale of hunting humans.

His ever-present acting collaborator Howard Vernon is here as Count Rabor Zaroff and *Countess Perverse*—Ivanna Zaroff—is portrayed by Alice Arno. The setting, an isolated island castle, is astounding. Franco's camerawork and the captivating sumptuous locale make for a visually striking film.

The film begins with a young couple rescuing a woman who has just washed up on the beach. To this pair she spills her story of the wretched encounter she has had with the Zaroffs.

Apparently she set out to rescue her sister from the wicked couple. The good news is that she finds her sister very soon after arriving at the Zaroff estate. The bad news is that her sister is the hunk of meat the Zaroffs are serving her at dinner after they have "so kindly" taken her in. Franco adds the travesty of cannibalism to the plot of the older movie.

Franco also adds rape and lesbianism to the mix. No surprise really, given the director's predilections. The woman in search of her sister is sexually assaulted the night of her arrival by none other than the perverse countess. Strangely, she finds herself swept up in the encounter, so the scene becomes transgressive and curiously erotic.

This scene also lets Franco display his love for the female form and for lusty Sapphic encounters. But Howard Vernon's Count Zaroff character is also involved in the encounter, though this heterosexual component does nothing to mitigate the beyond-the-pale nature of the situation—especially with the countess looking on and urging "Harder!"

Things take a turn for the even worse when a connection is revealed to exist between the Zaroffs and the young couple who "rescued" the unfortunate woman. The count is seen sending mirror signals across the water to the beachfront home where the couple lives.

The exact nature of the relationship between the couple and the Zaroffs remains unclear. But a bit of dialogue suggests that perhaps they are not entirely willing participants in the Count's nefarious schemes. Not that we should consider them innocents. They have their own perversities, as is soon made clear.

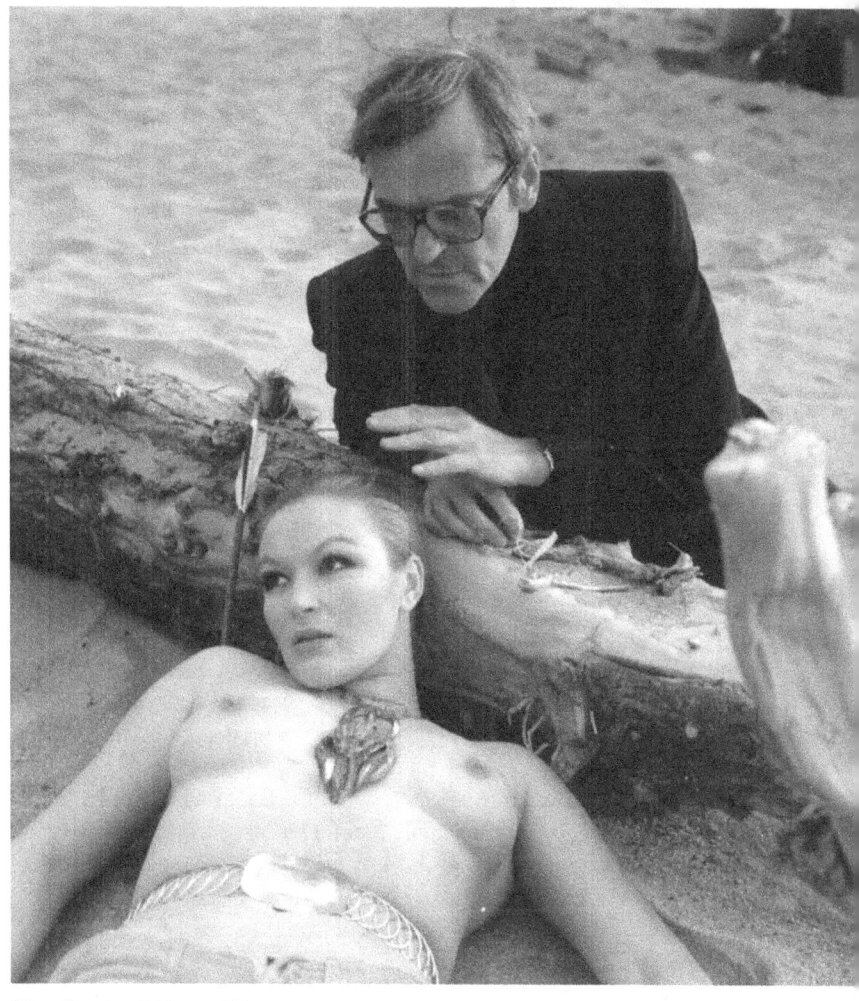

Alice Arno and Howard Vernon in *Countess Perverse*.

Not that a *ménage à trois* of willing participants (the third party being a lovely female friend of theirs) is a perversion. But in the context of all that is afoot, it does cause the viewer to look more closely at their character. It is not the act itself as much as it is their attitude toward the lover swapping in which they engage.

The couple takes their new friend for a boating excursion which ends up on a beach—a beach quite near the Zaroff estate. After some naked frolicking, they head for the peculiarly built Zaroff house. The new friend finds it spooky, as well she should. Next thing you know, the couple, their lady pal and the Zaroffs are seated around the dinner table and …

The conversation is tense, and laden with subtext. We know things the couple's new friend does not, yet the Zaroffs and their pair of willing or unwilling associates also seem privy, perhaps, to knowledge we the viewers do not have—even if such knowledge is no more than the exact nature of the relationship between the Zaroffs and their "friends." An earlier snippet of conversation has hinted that the relationship may not be entirely amicable.

At the very least, the film knows things about the near future we do not, and the dinner table scene helps to spike the suspense.

We then proceed to an unsurprising encounter between the countess and her new friend. The count watches, hidden, as the erotic play unfolds. This time there is no assault involved. The two women begin to kiss, caress and embrace with a full willingness on both sides.

Still, even in the midst of this amorousness the tension builds. Something wicked looms around the corner and the viewer is anxious to see the evil that awaits. Franco does a fine job of building tension in *Countess Perverse*.

For example, the very next scene shows the young, just-seduced friend awakening to strange noises, which she investigates. To her horror, she finds the source of the sound to be none other than Zaroff applying a saw to the corpse of a beautiful young dead woman. Here, the film elevates itself to a new plateau of horror.

The newcomer now knows exactly what the countess meant by her assertion that she adores the female form. Her lust is for far more than mere Eros. Through Thanatos, she also feeds the perverse lust of her belly. A simple image of the naked body of this woman behind a fan of flame is quite striking. Minus the flame it could be one of Franco's famous erotic shots.

And now as we stagger into the final reel, we see that the latest arrival's fear regarding the house in which she now finds herself is shown to have quite a real foundation. The count and countess explain to her the rules of their game. Their prey will have a head start.

And then the hunting begins.

(A surprise strangulation is also packed into this sequence when the male member of the Zaroffs' accomplice couple pins his naked wife to the bed and does the dirty deed.)

Meanwhile, the young woman is sent running—nude, of course—through the jungle accompanied by a tense psychedelic music score. Soon, Countess Zaroff is seen in pursuit. Fittingly, she is clothed with little more than a belt and necklace. The belt is a necessity as it holds a quiver of arrows for the bow clutched in her hand.

She is gorgeous and deadly. We almost wish she would catch us. Almost.

This chase sequence is a beautiful manifestation of Franco's comingling of Eros and Thanatos. We watch two attractive women running about in the buff—yet it is all in the name of a game of death. This sequence is a tense execution of one of the director's most pervasive themes.

(Meanwhile, the young man who throttled his wife is up to more antics of his own. Armed with his own bow, he is seen sneaking up to the Zaroff estate. We can only wonder what he has in mind.)

At the climax of the chase scene we see one of the film's most iconic shots: the naked Countess Zaroff down on one knee, in a firing position, placing an arrow in her bow and taking aim at her prey. The shot is fired and her arrow strikes the young woman.

But no sooner has the evil countess struck her target than the hunter becomes the hunted! The young man, whom we observed prowling the Zaroff estate, is targeting the countess herself. His shot is true and he fatally strikes her in the back in one of *Countess Perverse*'s premier cinematic shots—so to speak.

When the count (who has been spotting for his wife during the hunt) arrives on the scene, the young man threatens Zaroff with the authorities. But it is a hollow threat. His complicity in the Zaroffs' nasty deeds would not go over well with the police. So Zaroff walks away free, albeit without his wife.

However, a dead wife is not a tragedy for Zaroff, it seems, since his words, spoken over her body, reveal that his real lust for her is as the most delectable meal he could imagine.

Meanwhile, the grieving young man picks up the woman just killed by the countess and carries her into the sea, where he joins her in death.

I rank *Countess Perverse* among Franco's finer films. The film has his sense of headiness, but also features a surprisingly strong linear plot. In some ways, it is the best of both worlds. This film may not reach the heights of psychedelia that some of his more elliptical works achieve, but it is still fully Franco. And the story, with its twists and ironies, is one of his best tales. *Countess Perverse* also finds undiluted expression in the director's passion for coalescing the powers of Eros and Thanatos.

APPENDIX: ZOMBIE LAKE

Zombie Lake, is a peculiar—dare I say one of a kind—erotic horror film directed by Jean Rollin as "J.A. Laser." This film takes some standard Euro-sleaze material and bends it in a direction all its own. Somehow the movie emerges as an outstanding film, even when measured by the standards of its peers. Euro-horror, giallos and Eurotica had all evolved to be pretty wild and woolly forms already, when this quirky gem hit the screens in 1980.

Zombie Lake does so many of the things you would expect from an oversexed European horror film. There are zombie attacks—Nazi zombies, no less—copious graphic nudity, plus blood and all that, and even some smooth jazz music. But the tone and almost self-parodying demeanor of *Zombie Lake* is a whole other topic entirely.

While not strictly a Jess Franco film, this piece of truly gonzo cinema was written by Franco and directed by Jean Rollin (whom I consider sort of a French Franco, although I like Franco more). With that combination of talent, nothing sane or remotely normal—even perhaps by European genre film standards—could possibly have been expected to emerge on the silver screen.

I imagine even die-hard 42nd Street theatergoers were a mite surprised.

By conventional standards, this is anything but a good movie. This movie is not an exercise in realism—by any standard. It isn't trying to wow you with high tech gore-hound splatter. The film is a much more representational work than it is an attempt at verisimilitude.

You may have seen how on the stage a red ribbon will sometimes pass for a gout of blood? Well, I don't see why cinema can't have the option of "representing" events rather than always trying to duplicate reality (assuming the reality of Nazi zombies and such).

The first time a zombie munches on somebody's neck, the extremely simple effects are plain and obvious. Still, the low-tech representational style is a huge part of the charm of this movie. I very much doubt that auteurs Franco and Rollin were unaware of the look and feel of this bit of eye-goggling art house.

Before we witness the inexpensive, but effective (in this artistic context, at least) FX violence, there is the some real nudity and what a batch of nudity it is.

The credits appear over footage of a lone and none too shy woman stripping to the buff and going for a swim in the titular lake. By the way, this lake has a very daunting sign posted, warning all comers not to swim there. The sign even features the skull and crossbones symbol. Not that this exhibitionistic young lady gives a damn. The first thing she does when she gets to the sign is to yank it up and toss it aside.

Because screw anybody else who might like to know about the risks before hopping in!

At any rate, what ensues is a lily pad covered lake enjoying the skinny dipping of this young and well-built female. But of course she isn't the only thing in the lake taking a swim.

And I don't mean the fish or the ducks.

The swimmer is a zombie, of course. I guess he must have lain dormant until this beautiful babe happened along. Maybe the exact pattern of ripples caused by her flesh disturbing the water was of just the right vibration to wake the zombie up. Or maybe he was just patiently waiting around since everybody else since World War II (which plays a significant background role to the modern storyline of the film) has apparently had the good sense to pay attention to the sign.

Hope he likes 'em dumb, because this nude swimmer didn't come to the lake straight from a Mensa meeting.

When the zombie slowly raises his hand above water (*Deliverance*, anybody?), the first challenge to understanding/appreciating this movie has also raised its hand. The makeup appears to be nothing more than green paint slathered on the face and hands of the zombie and the water has already dissolved some of it.

At just this point, uninitiated viewers might pop a beer open and start laughing their asses off at this ludicrous example of shameless low camp.

Except that I don't think this film is low camp. I think this movie is an exercise in damn-the-torpedoes-full-speed-ahead filmmaking—movie craft for the sheer ecstasy of it. Again, there is no way in hell that Franco and Rollin are ignoring the "cheap" aspect of the film. That is why I declare that this movie is not low camp.

I am pretty sure that the immortal King of Camp Ed Wood was unaware that the films he was making were anything other than what he intended them to be, that is, making campy films was *not* his intent. But I find it hard to believe that Franco and Rollins were not perfectly aware of the camp value of *Zombie Lake*.

But back to our story. In no time the mayor of the small European village where these shenanigans are unfolding is made aware of the missing girl. Of course, everyone in the town is harboring the horror trope small town secret. They know the "lake of the damned" plus a missing hottie is NOT a good combination.

It soon follows that a woman in town is taken down by the zombie from the lake, whose appetites were clearly not sated by the skinny-dipping sweet young thing.

Next thing you know, we have slipped back into the past: an extended flashback begins to reveal some of the background behind current events. With a combination of Rollin-filmed footage using what few vehicular and costuming props were on hand, plus what I'm convinced is some borrowed stock footage of German tanks and infantrymen (no way did this movie have the dough for tanks), we see a Nazi blitzkrieg invasion of the village occurring at some time during World War II.

Amidst all the violence is a poor village woman caught in a small open field while artillery shells fall around her. A selfless and good-hearted German soldier leaps from his duck-and-cover spot on the ground and races over to protect her, getting himself injured in the process.

But something has happened during their brief encounter. It took Keanu Reeves and Sandra Bullock a whole bus ride to fall in love, but the village woman and the soldier make some kind of super duper emotional connection in the short time it takes him to save her life.

So after the soldier heals, he makes his way back to the village and finds her ready and willing in a barn. The lovemaking that follows is graphic but surprisingly tasteful, all things considered. We have a strange moment of tenderness in a movie that didn't really kick off promising such, and this won't be the last tender moment.

(Just wait until we get to the startling friendship that blossoms between a village girl and the aforementioned zombie.)

Meanwhile the flashback fighting continues.

I am not a war movie fan, but I have to say that I enjoyed seeing Rollin and Franco take a turn at using war scene footage in this peculiar context. The flashback scenes are almost as interesting as are those from the contemporary storyline.

And of course we aren't done with the man and woman who crossed enemy lines in the name of love. For love often bears its fruit and in this case, that means a baby was produced by the passionate lovemaking of these two whom the war threw together. Complications and more complications.

Considering that we already know that the woman's lover goes on to become a zombie, it's easy to surmise that this love story isn't going to end well for the two of them.

A group of villagers go guerilla and hunt down the Nazis—and I bet you can guess what happens to the German bodies. And it gets worse: the mother of the baby born from a dalliance with the enemy also dies. From childbirth? Grief?

It doesn't matter.

What does matter is that the German soldier (whose karma surely should have been better than this) ends up being gunned down by the villagers—despite his having saved one of their own, a rescue which in the end becomes only a nine-month reprieve.

We leave the flashback to jump forward for a brief look at the baby, who now appears to be in her teens. But we quickly skip across this scene and hop right into a van full women, all looking to do some skinny dipping of their own.

How lucky and unlucky are these villagers? Hot, nakedly inclined females seem to come bounding around on a regular basis, but there are also Nazi zombies hanging around the old swimmin' hole.

So here we are with another strip and swim scene that is a repeat of the first one we saw in the movie multiplied by however many of these beauties clown-car pop out of the van. And, again, the underwater shots give ample chance for the camera to get under the girls, meaning that everything short of actual cervix footage is on view—including—yikes!—the side of the swimming pool in which the film's "lake" swimming scenes were shot.

As is.

Oh, and more zombies are there too. So now all hell is really breaking loose and it seems that the village's secret may just fly out of the bag with lightning speed. Some bad PR for the small village will surely follow. And what chamber of commerce harboring a secret will stand for that?

The movie is already pushing some surreal components in terms of the way the film was shot. The deliberate disregard for executing some high-end Rick Baker or Rob Bottin gore effects, the blatant inclusion of footage that shows the side of a swimming pool—the overall counterintuitive abandoning of any sense of realism—makes this movie rather cinematically askew. Not to mention story plot point askew.

But, in addition, the film adds a helluva surrealist story twist that stands out as another major factor for most viewers writing this movie off as dreck—bad movie party dreck at best—but again I stipulate that what appear to be a gaping, mind-breaking script boo-boos cannot have escaped the awareness Franco and Rollins.

At last our first tender moment with a zombie has arrived. The little girl born of the coupling between villager and soldier is in her room when a zombie staggers in. The zombie not only does *not* make any attempt to eat her, but is actually quite sweet towards her.

The zombie is her father!

This fact is revealed when the zombie opens his uniform blouse to reveal the necklace he wears—of the same design as the one the soldier bestowed on his villager lady before his return to violence and soldiering.

The girl immediately recognizes the necklace and looks at a picture of her mother. Mr. Zombie Dad then removes the necklace from around his neck and puts it on the girl.

Very touching and not something you see in zombie movies.

But did you notice something?

Forty years removed from World War II, the zombie comes back—along with his less tender comrades—and visits his daughter—WHO IS BARELY EVEN A TEENAGER AND MAYBE NOT QUITE THAT OLD!

Yep.

For me however, this total rejection of linear continuity makes the movie that much more interesting. And fun.

Zombie Lake has the feel of being a satire; it is as if the movie is poking fun at all those generation-later, sins-of-the-father-visited-on-the-child horror thrillers where some fuck-up from the past comes back to inflict revenge on the next generation. It also feels like Franco and Rollins were trying to tell that kind of story and, well, Nazi zombies are way cooler than, say, Viet Cong zombies (though I suspect they would also be cool). And, besides, the only soldiers who would have been tearing up a French village in any remotely recent time would probably be the Germans, which brings us back to World War II.

But that's the thing. I do not believe that the filmmakers were even remotely concerned about credulity. This is a film about shock and sex-and-violence transgression through art, about atmosphere and mood, and in the end, about the hyper-joy of enthusiastic, dedicated moviemakers.

So back in the village things come to a head and we see the Angry Villagers vs. the Vengeful Dead.

Shades of Frankenstein and burning torches. And, as you may do with Frank, you are kind of rooting for the monsters.

And I actually find it hard not to love zombies created with nothing more than costumes and some runny green paint.

Zombie Lake is a truly unique walking dead picture. Truth be told, I'll take it over Romero or the entire *Walking Dead* TV series. Any day.

I love the film's conscious overturning of sane narrative and its marvelous willingness to tell its kooky story with minimal special effects. I find it sad that too few art fans (be it film or whatever) are blind to the beauty of minimalism.

This is a striking film and oodles more fun than most of the drek clogging the pipes in the zombie genre: so many of these films are about as animated and interesting as a single slogging slow-shuffler zombie itself.

It is also an engaging curiosity that the zombie dad and the girl almost become something akin to diplomats for each side of the human-zombie conflict. In fact, if loyalty were the issue on the table here, the zombie dad crosses the line even more blatantly than he did when saving and loving an enemy civilian.

As the climax of the film builds to whatever small-scale zombie apocalypse it has in store, the zombie father goes so far as to turn on his own zombie kind to save the girl from their blood-hungry intent. I'm sure it has happened elsewhere, somewhere, but zombie-on-zombie action is a rarity in the genre.

The daughter also takes a stand against the village leadership when they ask her to help out with the zombie outbreak, since they notice that she has a special connection—perhaps even a psychic one—with the dead.

Well, one of them, anyway.

Sure, she says, she will help the town get rid of them. But they can't hurt her zombie daddy. All the rest, sure. But not Daddy. The mayor assures her he just wants the best for everybody involved, zombies included. He wants to save the townsfolk and this can be done by giving the zombies a gift.

The gift of sleep, rest, a freedom from their zombie un-life.

Jaw-dropping continuity quirks aside, *Zombie Lake* spins a more interesting tale than you should have any right to expect from most zombie fodder. I don't even particularly care for the zombie genre. When I do love a zombie film, it must be something special.

Night of the Living Dead, for example. And if I have to justify that film's status as great cinema, you are just hopeless (even though I'm glad you are reading my book).

Also: Franco's *Oasis of the Zombies*. Nazi zombies again, and war flashbacks again. (Not that this film is the model for *Zombie Lake*.) But this time we have zombies in the desert with a lost treasure story attached. Or the same director's mysterious *Mansion of the Living Dead*, about zombie monks who will rape and kill you if you do bad things like, well, fuck. You'll get fucked for fucking. If you fuck, you're fucked. Egads! Both of these films are discussed elsewhere in the book, as you surely know unless you have been skipping around. Which is fine; I don't mind.

And thank you for joining me!

Jess Franco Films
(all as director except where noted)

1955
El Coyote (co-screenplay only)

1956
Coyote (co-writer only)
Miedo (co-writer only)
La melodía misteriosa (story only - as A.L. Mariaux)

1957
El árbol de España (Documentary short; co-screenplay/story only)
Fulano y Mengano (writer only)

1959
Luna de verano (writer only)
Las playas vacías (Documentary short; screenplay/story only)
Llegaron los franceses (writer only)
Oro español (Documentary short; co-screenplay/story only)
We're Eighteen (Tenemos 18 Años; directorial debut, also screenplay)

1960
Red Lips (Labios Rojos; also as Operation Levres Rouge / Operation Red Lips)
Queen of the Tabarin Club (La Reina del Tabarin; also as Mariquita la Belle de Tabarin)

1961
Vampiresas 1930 (Volando Hacia la Fama / Flying Towards Fame; also as Gold Diggers of 1930 and Certains les preferent noires/ Some Like it Black)
The Awful Dr. Orloff (Gritos en la Noche / Screams in the Night; also as El doctor demonio / The Demon Doctor, L'Horrible Dr. Orlof, Il Diabolico Dottor Satana, Der Schreckliche Dr. Orlof)

1962
Death Whistles the Blues (La Muerte Silba Un Blues; also as Agent 077 Operation Jamaique and 077 Operation Sexy; remade by Franco in 1973 as Kiss Me Killer)
The Shadow of Zorro(La sombra del Zorro; also as La venganza del Zorro, La Espada del Zorro; screenplay only)
The Sadistic Baron Von Klaus (Le sadique baron von Klaus, also as La Mano de un Hombre Muerto/ Hand of a Dead Man, Le Sadique/ The Sadist, Hysterical Sadique, La Bestia del Castello Maldetto / Beast of the Cursed Castle and Sinfonia Per Un Sadico / Symphony for a Sadist)

1963
Rififi in the City (Rififi en la ciudad / Rumble in the City; also as Vous souvenez vous de Paco? / Do You Remember Paco?, Chasse a la Maffia / Hunt for the Mafia and Una Spia Sulla Cita/ A Spy in the City)
The Jaguar (El Llanero / The Plainsman; also as Sfida Selvaggio / Savage Challenge and Le Jaguar)

1964
El Extraño Viaje (The Strange Journey; actor only)
The Secret of Dr. Orloff (El Secreto del Dr. Orloff; also as Le Amanti del Dottor Jekyll / The Lovers of Dr. Jekyll / Die Geliebten des Dr. Jekyll, Dr. Orloff's Monster [AIP's 1966 dubbed U.S. TV print] and Les Maitresses du Dr. Jekyll / The Mistresses of Dr. Jekyll, a French version with a few scenes added by Franco in 1965)

1965
Treasure Island (La Isla del Tesoro, unfinished; this film was supposed to star Orson Welles as Long John Silver, Sir John Gielgud & Fernando Rey; screenplay by Welles)
Chimes at Midnight (Campanadas a Medianoche, also as Falstaff [U.S. release title] with Orson Welles, Jeanne Moreau, Sir John Gielgud and Fernando Rey; Franco was 2nd unit director),
The Diabolical Dr. Z(Miss Muerte / Miss Death; also as Le Diabolique Docteur Z, Dans les Griffes du Maniaque / In the Grip of the Maniac and Das Geheimnis des Dr. Z / The Secret of Dr. Z)
077 Intrigue in Lisbon (Espionage in Lisbon;

also as Mision Lisboa; Franco co-wrote only)

1966

Attack of the Robots(Cartas Sur Table / Cards on the Table; also as Cartas Boca Arriba / Cards Face Up, James Clint Challenges Interpol / James Clint sfida Interpol and Karten auf den Tisch)

Residence for Spies (Residencia Para Espias; also as Les Mignonnes / The Darlings and Golden Horn)

Lucky, the Inscrutable (Lucky el Intrepido; also as Agente Speciale L.K., Operation Re Mida / Operation King Midas and Corrida Pour un Espion / Race For a Spy)

1967

Necronomicon (Necronomicon Getraumte Sunden / Necronomicon Dreamt Sin; also as Delirium and Succubus, the 1971 English language edit)

Red Lips Sadisterotica (Rote Lippen Sadisterotica, also as El Caso de las Dos Bellezas / The Case of the Two Beauties, Two Avenging Angels, Der Wolf-Horror Pervers and Two Undercover Angels - U.S. title)

Kiss Me Monster (Besame Monstruo, also as Das Schloss der Gehenkten / Castle of the Hanged Men and Castle of the Doomed)

In the Castle of Bloody Lust(Im Schloss der Blutigen Begierde, also as Castle of Lust and Castle of the Creeping Flesh [U.S. title]; original plot by Franco only)

1968

The Blood of Fu Manchu (Fu Manchu y el Beso de la Muerte / Fu Manchu and the Kiss of Death; also as Der Todeskuss des Dr. Fu Manchu / The Death Kiss of Dr. Fu Manchu, Sax Rohmer's Kiss and Kill and Against All Odds - U.S. video title)

The Girl from Rio (La Ciudad sin Hombres / City Without Men; also as Sumuru Regina di Femina / Sumuru, Queen of Femina, Die Sieben Männer der Su-Muru / The Seven Men of Su-Muru, Rio 70, Future Women [U.S. TV title] and Mothers of America)

99 Women (99 Mujeres / 99 Donne / 99 Frauen; also as Der Heisse Tod / Hot Death, 99 Femmes Perverses, Island of Despair [edited U.S. TV version] and Les Brulantes / The Burning Women, the 1974 French hardcore version)

Eve (Eva en la Selva / Eve in the Jungle, also as The Face of Eve, La Femmina della Giungla and Diana, Daughter of the Wilderness; Franco was an uncredited co-director)

Marquis de Sade: Justine (Les Infortunes de la Vertu / The Misfortunes of Virtue; also as Justine and Juliet, Las Dos Bellezas / The Two Beauties, Dulce Justine / Sweet Justine and Deadly Sanctuary - 1986 U.S. video title)

The Castle of Fu Manchu (El Castillo de Fu Manchu, also as Der Folterkammer des Dr. Fu Manchu/ The Torture Chamber of Dr. Fu Manchu and Assignment Istanbul)

Venus in Furs(Venus im Pelz; also as Black Angel, Puo una morta revivere per amore? / Can a Dead Girl Live Again Through Love? and Paroxismus)

1969

Eugenie, The Story of Her Journey into Perversion (Die Jungfrau und die Peitsche / The Virgin and the Whip, De Sade 70: Beaten and Loved, Les Inassouvies / The Insatiables and Philosophy in the Boudoir; remade as Cocktail Special in 1978)

The Bloody Judge (El Juez Sangriento, also as El Proceso de las Brujas / The Trial of the Witches, Il Truono di Fuoco / Throne of Fire, Der Hexentöter von Blackmoor / The Witch-Killer of Blackmoor, De Sadistiche Rechter, El poder del fuego and Night of the Blood Monster - U.S. theatrical title)

Count Dracula (El Conde Dracula / Il conte Dracula; also as Nachts wenn Dracula erwacht / Nights When Dracula Wakes, Le nuits de Dracula / The Nights of Dracula, Bram Stoker's Count Dracula, Bloodthirsty Dracula and Dracula '71)

Sex Charade(Like an Apocalypse; also as The

Labyrinth; finished but never released)
Nightmares Come at Night (Les Cauchemars Naissent la Nuit, also as Les yeux de la Nuit / Los Ojos de la Noche/ The Eyes of the Night, Die Nackten Augen der Nacht and Sangre en la noche; remade by Franco in 1972 as The Sinister Eyes of Dr. Orloff)

1970

Eugenie de Sade (Eugenie (De Sade); also as Eugenie, Eugenia, De Sade 2000, Eugenie de Franval and Eugenie Sex Happening)

Vampyros Lesbos (Erbin des Dracula / The Heiress of Dracula, also as Sexualite Speciale, Las Vampiras and El Signo del Vampiro); remade by Franco in 1981 as Macumba Sexual)

She Killed in Ecstasy(Sie Tötete in Ekstase; also as Mrs. Hyde, Crimes dans l'extase / Crimes of Ecstasy and Lewd in Ecstasy)

The Devil Came from Akasava (El Diablo que vino de Akasava, also as Der Teufel kam aus Akasava, The Devils of Caninde and Una venere senza nome per L'ispettore Forrester / A Nameless Love for Inspector Forrester)

Juliette (Juliette de Sade; never completed due to Soledad Miranda's untimely death in 1970)

X-312 Flight to Hell (X312 - Flug zur Hölle, also as Vuelo al Infierno, Die Grüne Hölle des Amazonas / The Green Hell of the Amazon, Infierno, tuya es la victoria / Hell...You Win and Amazonas)

1971

The Death Avenger of Soho(Der Todesrächer von Soho, also as El Muerto Hace las Maletas / The Corpse Packs his Bags, The Avenger and Allarme a Scotland Yard: Sei Omicidi Senza Assassino)

The Revenge of Dr. Mabuse(La Venganza del Dr. Mabuse, also as Mabuse 70, El Dr. Mabuse, Dr. M schlägt zu / Dr. M Strikes Back and The Man Who Called Himself Mabuse)

Virgin Report(Jungfrauen Report, also as Le Vierges et l'Amour / Virgins and Love and Defloration; sex documentary)

Three Naked Women on Robinson Island (Trois Filles Nues dans L'Ile de Robinson, also as Robinson und seine Wilden Sklavinnen / Robinson and his Wild Slaves, Sexy Darlings and The Island of Forbidden Pleasures)

A Virgin Among the Living Dead (released in 1973; Une Vierge chez les Morts Vivant, Una Vergine tra gli Zombi, Christina princesse de l'erotisme / Christina, Princess of Eroticism, I desideri erotici di Christine, The Erotic Dreams of Christine, A Young Girl Among the Living Dead, Exorcismo per una Vergine and La Nuit des Etoiles Filantes / The Night of the Shooting Stars); re-released with added zombie footage, filmed by Jean Rollin, in 1981)

Blood on the Shoes (Sangre en los zapatos; unfinished)

Dracula vs. Frankenstein (Dracula Contra Frankenstein, also as Dracula, Prisonier de Frankenstein / Dracula, Prisoner of Frankenstein, Die Nacht der Offenen Särge / The Night of the Open Coffins and The Screaming Dead - U.S. video title)

1972

Daughter of Dracula(La Fille de Dracula / Da vloek van Dracula)

The Lovers of Devil's Island(Los Amantes de la Isla del Diablo, also as Violences erotiques dans une prison de femmes / Erotic Violence in a Women's Prison, Quartier de femmes and Devil's Island Lovers)

The Curse of Frankenstein (La Maldicion de Frankenstein; also as The Erotic Rites of Frankenstein and Les Exploits Erotiques de Frankenstein / The Erotic Experiences of Frankenstein)

The Demons(Les Demons, also as The She-Demons, Die Nonnen von Clichy / The Nuns of Clichy, Les Demons du Sexe / The Demons of Sex, Les Infants du Demon / Children of the Demon, Os Demonios and Les novices perverses)

A Captain of Fifteen Years(Un Capitan de Quince Anos)

Relax, Baby(Un Tiro en la Sien / A Bullet in the Head; unreleased, apparently unfinished)

Mystery of the Red Castle (Misterio del Castillo Rojo; unreleased, apparently unfinished)

A Silence of the Grave (Un silencio de tumba)

Intimate Diary of a Nymphomaniac (Le Journal Intime d'une Nymphomane, also as Sinner, Diary of a Nymphomaniac and Les Inassouvies 77 / The Insatiables '77)

The House of Vice (La Maison du Vice . Dolls For Sale, also as Les Ebranlees / The Vibrating Girls and Des Filles Pour L'Amour / Women for Love)

The Sinister Eyes of Dr. Orloff (Los ojos siniestros del Dr. Orloff, also as Los ojos del Dr. Orloff; a remake of Nightmares Come At Night)

1973

Pleasure For Three (Plaisir a Trois, also as How To Seduce a Virgin and Les Innasouvies II / The Insatiables Part 2; remade by Franco in 1979 as Erotic Symphony)

The Perverse Countess (Le Comtesse Perverse, also as Un Caldo Corpo di Femina / The Warm Body of a Woman, The Countess Zaroff, Sexy Nature and Les Croqueuses / The Munchers; remade by Franco in 1997 as Tender Flesh)

The Other Side of the Mirror(Al Otro Lado del Espejo, also as Le Miroir Cochon, Outre-Tombe / Ultra Tumba, Lo Specchio del Piacere / The Mirror of Pleasure, Inceste and Le Miroir Obscene / The Obscene Mirror)

Maciste vs. the Amazon Queen (Maciste Contre la Reine des Amazones, also as The Lustful Amazons, Les Amazones de la Luxure, Maciste aux Mains des Amazones Nues, Karzan Contro le Donne dal Seno Nudo / Karzan vs. the Bare-Breasted Women and Yuka)

The Erotic Exploits of Maciste in Atlantis (Les Exploits Erotiques de Macist dans L'Atlantide, also as Les Gloutonnes / The Gobblers and Sexes au Soleil)

The Bare-Breasted Countess (released in 1975; La Comtesse Aux Seins Nus, La Comtesse Noire / The Black Countess, The Loves of Irina, Erotikill, Les Avaleuses / The Swallowers, Entfesselte Begierde / Unbridled Lust and Female Vampire, the DVD title)

Night of the Killers (La Noche de los Asesinos / Night of the Assassins, also as Night of the Skull [DVD title], Sospiri and Im Schatten des Mörders / In the Shadow of Murder)

La Casa del Ahorcado (The House of the Hanged Man and Le Manoir du Pendu;unfinished)

Linda's Hot Nights (Les Nuits Brulantes de Linda, also as La Felicita nel Peccato / The Felicity of Sin, Le Plaisir Solitaire / Solitary Pleasure and Mais Que Donc a Viole Linda? / Who Raped Linda?; remade by Franco in 1977 as Sexy Sisters)

Tender and Perverse Emanuelle (Tender et Perverse Emmanuelle, also as Des Frissons sur la Peau / Shivers of the Flesh, Le Chemin Solitaire / The Solitary Path, El Ultimo Escalofrio / The Last Thrill and Dernier Frisson)

Kiss Me, Killer (Sexy Blues, Tango au Clair de Lune / Tango by Moonlight, Emanuelle Blonde, Come With Me My Blonde Emmanuelle, Embrasse-Moi and Dolce Porno Baby; a remake of Franco's 1962 film, Death Whistles the Blues)

The Mark of Zorro (La marque de Zorro; released in 1975)

1974

Exorcisme (Exorcisme et Messes Noires / Exorcism and Black Masses, also as Le Viziose and Sexorcismes; footage from this film was later re-edited into Franco's 1979 Sadist of Notre Dame)

Celestine, Maid at Your Service (Celestine, Bonne a Tout Faire / Celestine, Good for

Anything, also as. Celestine, an All-Around Maid; remade by Franco in 1984 as Scarlet)
Lorna, the Exorcist (Lorna, l'Exorciste, also as Les Possedees du Diable / The Devil's Possessed and Sexy Diabolic Story; remade by Franco in 2002 as Jess Franco's Incubus)
Nuns in Madness (Les Nonnes en Folie, also as Les Chatouilleuses / The Ticklish Ones and Le sexy goditrici / God's Sexy Women)
The Sexiest Man in the World (also as Sexy Erotic Job, Le Jouisseur / The Hedonist, Roland, L'Homme le Plus Sexy du Monde and Der Sex Playboy)
Les Emmerdeuses (The Troublemakers, also as Les Grandes Emmerdeuses / The Big Pains in the Ass and Sexy-a-Go-Go)
Convoy of Women (also as East of Berlin, Convoy of Girls and SS Nazi Convoy; Franco apparently co-directed this film [uncredited] with Pierre Chevalier, although some sources dispute it)

1975

De Sade's Juliette (also as Justine Lady Lujuria, Julietta 69 and Justine)
Midnight Party (Le Partouze de Minuit, also as Heisse Berührungen, Lady Porno, La Coccolona, Sexy Blues, Porno Pop and Porno Dama)
Shining Sex (Le Sexe Brillant, also as La Fille au Sexe Brillant / The Girl With the Shining Sex and Erotic Pleasures of a Good Lady)
Women in a Golden Cage (Des Filles dans une Cage Doree, also as Razzia Sur le Plaisir, Vizio in Bocca and Carcel Dorada; co-directed by Marius Lesoeur)
Mandinga (Mandinga; unfinished film)
A Virgin for St. Tropez (Une vierge pour Saint-Tropez: Franco helped Georges Friendland direct this film, uncredited)
Barbed Wire Dolls (also as Frauengefängnis / Women's Prison. Caged Women and Penitenziario Femminile per Reali Sessuali)
Women Behind Bars (also as Diamants Pour L'Enfer / Diamonds for Hell, Visa Pour Mourir / Visa To Die, Prison Sado Pour Femmes / Sadistic Women's Prison and Punition Cell)
The Man From Guyane (L'Homme de la Guyane; unfinished film that was supposed to star Orson Welles and Klaus Kinski)
Downtown: The Naked Dolls of the Underworld (Downtown Die Nackten Puppen der Unterwelt, also as Les putains de la ville basse/ The Whores of the Underworld, Levres Rouge et Bottes Noires and Schwarze Nylons, Wilde Engel)
The Slaves (Die Sklavinnen, also as Die Verschleppten / The Neglected Ones and Les Flagellees de la Cellule 69)

1976

The Portrait of Doriana Gray(Das Bildnis der Doriana Gray, also as Die Marquise de Sade, Dirty Dracula, Ejaculations and La Porno Storia della Marchesa De Sade)
Girls of the Night Shift (Mädchen im Nachtverkehr, also as Wilde Lust / Wild Lust and Heiber Sex in Nachtverkehr)
White Skin, Black Thigh (Weisse Haut auf Schwarzen Schenkeln; sex film in which Franco only acted)
Jack the Ripper (Jack l'Eventreur, also as Erotico Profondo and Jack the Ripper, der Dirnenmörder von London)
Around the World in 80 Beds (In 80 Betten um die Welt)
Greta, the Mad Butcher (Greta Haus Ohne Männer / Greta, House Without Men, also as Ilsa, Ultimate Power, Ilsa, the Wicked Warden, Greta la Tortionnaire de Wrede / Greta The Torturer, Wanda the Wicked Warden and Greta la Donna Bestia)
Love Letters of a Portuguese Nun (Die Liebesbriefe einer Portugiesischen Nonne, also as Forbidden Confessions of an Adolescent Nun and Cartas de Amor a Una Monja Portuguesa)

1977

Das Frauenhaus (The Women's House, also as House of Women and Blue Rita)
Sexy Sisters (Die Teuflischen Schwestern / The Devilish Sisters, also as Satanic

Sisters, Two Vicious Sisters, Swedish Nympho Slaves, Aberraciones Sexuales de una Rubia Caliente / Sexual Aberrations of a Hot Blonde and Erotic Frenzy of a Nymphomaniac)

Women Without Innocence (Frauen Ohne Unschuld, also as Wicked Women, The Insatiable Nights of a Nymphomaniac and Femmes Sans Pudeur / Women Without Modesty

Love Camp (Camp d'Amour, also as Frauen im Liebeslager / Women in the Love Camp, Camp Erotique and Die Unersattliche)

The Call of the Blonde Goddess (Ruf der Blonden Göttin, also as Las Diosas del Porno / The Goddesses of Porn, La Deesse Nue / The Naked Goddess, Porno Shock, Love Cry of the Blonde Goddess and Voodoo Passion)

Women in Cellblock 9 (Frauen für Zellenblock 9, also as Esclaves de l'Amour/ Love Slaves and· Flucht von der Todesinsel)

1978

Cocktail Special

Elles Font Tout (They Do It All, also as They Do Everything and Quel Certo Piacere; remade by Franco in 1982 as El hotel de los ligues)

I'm Burning Up All Over (Je Brule de Partout, also as Dossier Mineures)

Two Female Spies with Flowered Panties (Deux Espionnes Avec un Petit Slip a Fleur, also as Opalo de Fuego: Mercarderes del Sexo / Opal of Fire: The Sex Merchants and Lascivia)

1979

Erotic Symphony (Sinfonia Erotica, also as Cuerpos y Almas / Bodies and Souls; remake of Franco's 1973 film Pleasure for Three)

The Girls of Copacabana (Las Chicas de Copacabana, also as Las Muchachas de Copacabana)

The Sadist of Notre Dame (El Sadico de Notre Dame, also as Le Sadique de Notre Dame, The Ripper of Notre Dame, Chains and Black Leather and Demoniac – the censored U.S. video release)

The Gold Bug(El escarabajo de oro;unfinished)

1980

Sexual Aberrations of a Married Woman (Aberraciones Sexuales de una Mujer Casada, also as Diary of a Desperate Housewife, Sexual Aberrations of a Housewife and Cecilia)

Eugenie: The Story of a Perversion (Eugenie Historia de una Perversion, also as The Wicked Memoirs of Eugenie, Erotismo and Lolita am Scheideweg)

Mondo Cannibale (Cannibal World, also as Les Cannibales / The Cannibals, La Dea Cannibale / The Cannibal Goddess, White Cannibal Queen, Die Blonde Gottin /The Blonde Goddess, Barbarian Goddess, Une Fille Pour Les Cannibales / A Woman for the Cannibals and Rio Salvaje)

Cannibal Terror (Terreur Cannibal; screenplay only; incorporated footage from Franco's Mondo Cannibale, 1980)

Devil Hunter(Chasseurs d'Hommes, also as Man Hunter, Sexo Cannibal, Jungfrau unter Kannibalen / The Young Woman and the Cannibals and Mandingo Manhunter - USA video title)

Zombie Lake(also as El lago de los muertos vivientes / The Lake of the Living Dead and Le lac des morts-vivant; Jean Rollins directed from Franco's screenplay)

Sadomania: The Hell of Passion (Sadomania: El Infierno de la Pasion, also as Sadomania, Hölle der Lust, Hellhole Women and Prisoners of the Flesh)prison film co-produced by Antonio Mayans & Julio Poura; written by Franco & Gunter Ebert; co-directed by Lina Romay & Franco; starred Ajita Wilson (a real-life transsexual), Antonio Mayans, Ursula Buchfellner, Nadine Pascal & Jesus Franco

Bloody Moon(Lune de Sang, also as Die Säge des Todes/ The Saw of Death, Profonde Tenebre / Deep Darkness and

Colegiadas Violadas / Raped College Girls; co-directed by Lina Romay & Franco)

The Naked Superwitches of the Rio Amore(Die Nackten Superhexen vom Rio Amore, also as Die Frauen vom Rio Amore, Orgia de Ninfomanas, Captive Women [video title] and The Story of Linda [UK title], this version co-directed by Franco & Lina Romay)

Sex Is Crazy(El Sexo Esta Loco)

The Girl in the Transparent Panties (La Chica de las Bragas Transparentes, also as Pick-up Girls and Two Females Spies With Flowered Panties)

1981

Lake of the Virgins (El Lago de los Virgenes, also aso Island of the Virgins)

The Night of the Open Sexes(La noche de los sexos abiertos)

Kalt wie Eis(Strike Back; Franco helped Carl Schenkel direct this film, uncredited)

Macumba Sexual (Sexual Voodoo; remake of Franco's 1970 film Vampyros Lesbos)

Oasis of the Zombies(L'Abime des Morts Vivants / The Abyss of the Living Dead, also as Bloodsucking Nazi Zombies [video title] and Le Tresor des Morts Vivants / Treasure of the Living Dead)

1982

Intimate Confessions of an Exhibitionist (Confesiones íntimas de una exhibicionista)

Black Boots, Leather Whip (Botas Negras, Latigo de Cuerostarred)

The Sinister Dr. Orloff (El Siniestro Dr. Orloff, also as Experimentos Macabros / Macabre Experiments)

The Inconfessable Orgies of Emanuelle (also as Emanuelle Exposed and Emanuelle's Secret Orgies)

El hotel de los ligues(The Hotel of Rendezvous, also as The Hotel of Love Affairs; remake of Franco's Elles Font Tout, 1978)

The House of the Lost Women (La Casa de las Mujeres Perdidas, also as Perversion en la Isla Perdida / Perversion on the Lost Island)

Mansion of the Living Dead(La Mansion de los Muertos Vivientes)

The Shadow of Judoka vs. Dr. Wong (La Sombra del Judoka contra el Dr. Wong)

Moans of Pleasure (Gemidos de Placer; remake of Franco's Pleasure For Three, 1973)

1983

Fury in the Tropics (Furia en el Tropico, also as Orgasmo Perverso, Mujeres Acorraladas / Cornered Women and Fury in Jamaica)

Treasure of the White Goddess (El Tesoro de la Diosa Blanca, also as Diamonds of Kilimandjaro - DVD title)

Revenge in the House Of Usher (Die Rache des Hauses Usher, also as El Hundimiento de la Casa Usher / The Fall of the House of Usher, Nevrosis / Neurosis, Los Crimenes de Usher / The Crimes of Usher and Zombie 5)

The Night Has a Thousand Sexes (Mil Sexos Tiene La Noche)

Lillian the Perverted Virgin (Lilian la Virgen Pervertida)

The Sexual Story of O (La Historia Sexual de O, also as Lola 2000 and Une petite femme pour hotel particulier)

Alone Against Terror(Sola Ante el Terror, also as Los Monstruos de Fiske Manor/ The Monsters of Fiske Manor)

Blood On My Shoes (Sangre en mis Zapatos)

The Blues of Pop Street (Los Blues de la Calle Pop, also as Las Aventuras de Felipe Marlboro Volumen Ocho / The Adventures of Phillip Marlboro, Volume 8 and The Pop Street Blues)

In Search of the Golden Dragon (En Busca del Dragon Dorado)

Camino Solitario (Lonely Road)

Barrio Chino (Barrio Porno; unreleased)

The Tanga Girls (Las Chicas del Tanga; supposedly directed by Lina Romay)

A Buttcrack for Two (Una Rajita Para Dos / A Crack For Two; Lina Romay's first solo directing job; Franco as actor)

1984
How Much Does a Spy Cost? (Cuanto Cobra un Espia?)
Dirty Game in Casablanca (Juego Sucio en Casablanca)
The Girl with the Red Lips (La Chica de los Labios Rojos)
Golden Temple Amazons (Les Amazones du Temple d'Or, also as Tundra and the Temple of the Sun; started by Franco as Tundra in 1984 but never completed, finished by Alain Petit and released in 1990 as Golden Temple Amazons)
White Bay (Bahia Blanca)
The Killer Wore Black Socks(El asesino llevaba medias negras; unfinished)
Voices of Death (Voces de Muerte, also as Finestrat; unfinished)
Scarlet(also as The Grandfather, the Countess and Mischievous Scarlet and Escarlate la Traviesa / Naughty Scarlet; remake of Franco's Celestine, 1974, but never released)

1985
The White Slave (La Esclava Blanca)
Lulu's Talking Ass (El Ojete de Lulu [Lulu's Buttonhole], also as Lulu's Bunghole)
Lulu's Pacifier(El Chupete de Lulu, also as Lulu's Suck Toy)
A Penis for Three (Un Pito Para Tres / A Whistle For Three; co-directed and written by Lina Romay)
Last of the Filipinas (Las Ultimas de Filipinas; co-directed by Lina Romay)
Bangkok: Appointment with Death (Bangkok, cita con la muerte)
Travel to Bangkok, Coffin Included(Viaje a Bangkok Ataud Incluido)
Commando Mengele (Angel of Death, also as El Hombre que Mato a Mengele and Gentes del Rio; co-writer only)
Entre pitos anda el juego (The Play Moves Between Penises, also as The Game Walks Between Whistles)

1986
The Watcher and the Exhibitionist (El Miron y la Exhibicionista / The Voyeur and the Exhibitionist; co-directed by Lina Romay)
Slaves of Crime (Esclavas del Crimen)
The Suckers (Las Chuponas; co-directed by Lina Romay)
For The Babies, Warm Cream (Para Las Nenas Leche Calentita; co-directed by Lina Romay)
Tribulations of a Cross-Eyed Buddha (Tribulaciones de un Buda Bizco; a children's film, completed but never released)
AIDS: the 20th Century Plague (Sida, la Peste del Siglo XX, also as Operation Sida; completed but apparently lost)
Teleporno (unfinished hardcore film)
The White Rhino (El rinoceronte blanco, also as Revenge of the White Rhino; unfinished)
Bragueta Story (Zipper Story; unreleased; directed by Lina Romay)

1987
Falo Crest (also as Caprices Sados Pour Salopes du Plaisir / Sadistic Whims for Whores of Pleasure and Phallo Crest; co-directed by Lina Romay; x-rated parady of Falconcrest)
Phollastia (also as Fellations Sauvages / Wild Fellatio; co-directed by Lina Romay; x-rated parody of Dynasty)
Biba La Banda (producer only)
Dark Mission (Fleurs du Mal / Flowers of Evil, also as The Columbian Connection, Operacion Cocaina and The Heroin Deal)

1988
Faceless (also as Les Predateurs de la Nuit / Predators of the Night and I Predatori della Notte; an homage to Franco's The Awful Dr. Orloff)

1989
Emerald Bay (La Bahia Esmeralda, also as Esmeralda Bay)

1990
The Fall of Eagles (La Chute des Aigles, also as Un Cancion Para Berlin / A Song for Berlin and War Song)
Downtown Heat (Ciudad Baja, also as Vipers and La punta de las viboras / Viper's

Point; released in 1994)
In Pursuit of Barbara (À la Poursuite de Barbara; co-directed with Jean Rollin)

1992
Don Quijote (completion of a film started by Orson Welles in 1957 as a projected TV series; released in 1995)

1993
Jungle of Fear(La Jungla del Miedo, also as The Golden Beetle; unfinished)

1996
Killer Barbys(also as Vampire Killer Barbys and Killer Barbies; Franco's last big-budget film)

1997
Tender Flesh (Carne Fresca, also as Bocatto di Cardinale; remake of Franco's The Perverse Countess, 1973)

1998
Mari-Cookie and the Killer Tarantula (Mari Cookie y la tarantula asesina, also as Eight Legs To Love You)
Lust for Frankenstein

1999
Dr. Wong's Virtual Hell (El infierno virtual del Dr. Wong, also as Doctor Wong)
Vampire Blues (Los blues del vampire, also as Vampire Sex: Lady Dracula 3 and Vampyr Blues)
Red Silk (Seda Roja)
Broken Dolls (Munecas Rotas)

2000
Helter Skelter
Blind Target (Obietivo a Ciegas)

2001
Vampire Junction

2002
Jess Franco's Incubus(also as Incubus; remake of Franco's Lorna the Exorcist, 1974)

Antenna Criminal: Making a Jess Franco Movie (documentary on the making of Blind Target, directed by Brian Horrorwitz)
The Killer Barbys vs. Dracula (Killer Barbys Contra Dracula)

2005
Flowers of Perversion(also as Jess Franco's Perversion and Flores de perversion)
Flowers of Passion (also as Jess Franco's Passion and Flores de la Pasion)
Snakewoman

2008
A Bad Day at the Cemetery, Parts 1 & 2 (also as La cripta de las mujeres malditas / Crypt of the Cursed Women; filmed in two parts: Part one was released in 2008, Part two was released in 2010)

2009
Take-Away Spirit

2010
Paula-Paula: An Audiovisual Experience (also as Paula-Paula; Lina Romay's last film)

2012
Al Pereira vs. the Alligator Women (also as Culitos in the Night and Al Pereira vs. the Alligator Ladies)
Crypt of the Condemned, Parts One and Two (La cripta de las condenadas 1 & 2)

2013
Revenge of the Alligator Women (also as Revenge of the Alligator Ladies)

References:
Wikipedia [Thrower,Stephen *Murderous Passions: The Delirious Cinema of Jesus Franco*. Strange Attractor Press, 2015]
IMDb

Kristofer Upjohn has wanted to be a writer since he was in junior high school. He has loved strange cinema longer than that. He spent a decade in newspaper journalism, acquired a B.S. in psychology with a background in mathematics, and blogs about movies, music and books, and podcasts regularly. Upjohn has penned and published five books previously through his one-man publishing imprint, Book Devil Press. He has interviewed several horror and music celebrities. He is at work on a second book for Stark House Press. More of his writings may be found at bookdevil.tumblr.com, noirjournal.tumblr.com, filmphreak.tumblr.com and audioasshole.tumblr.com.

www.ingramcontent.com/pod-product-compliance
Lightning Source LLC
Chambersburg PA
CBHW071618080526
44588CB00010B/1171